INTEGRATIVE LEARNING AS THE PATHWAY TO TEACHING HOLISM, COMPLEXITY AND INTERCONNECTEDNESS

Edited by

Billie Goode Blair

and

Renate N. Caine

EMText
Lewiston/Queenston/Lampeter

Library of Congress Cataloging-in-Publication Data

Integrative learning as the pathway to teaching holism, complexity,
   and interconnectedness / edited by Billie Goode Blair and Renate N.
Caine.
        p.   cm.
   Includes bibliographical references.
   ISBN 0-7734-9153-8 (paper)
      1. Learning, Psychology of. 2. Teaching. 3. Cognitive learning.
I. Blair, Billie G. II. Caine, Renate Nummela.
LB1060.I557   1995
370.15'23--dc20   94-40518
                                                                                CIP

A CIP catalog record for this book is available from the British Library.

The Edwin Mellen Press   The Edwin Mellen Press
         Box 450   Box 67
Lewiston, New York   Queenston, Ontario
   USA 14092-0450   CANADA L0S 1L0

The Edwin Mellen Press, Ltd.
Lampeter, Dyfed, Wales
UNITED KINGDOM SA48 7DY

Printed in the United States of America

Table of Contents

INTEGRATIVE LEARNING: EMERGING PERSPECTIVES

Introduction

Members of the Center for Research in Integrative Learning and Teaching form a unique group. Center members represent a variety of backgrounds, educational experiences and professional disciplines. We meet and converse frequently, hold periodic research discussions open to all faculty, and retreat, every six months or so, to the San Gorgonio mountains for reassessment, rethinking, planning and revitalization.

It is from this group and from the continued inspiration which this group gives to its members that these papers have emerged. The papers reflect what we are: a variety of approaches and thinking united around a central theme. The focus of the center is on integrative learning and integrative education. Each center member approaches the theme differently from the orientation of curriculum, psychology, sociology, linguistics, math, science, history, evaluation, or administration. Yet, we are united in believing that education of the future must embrace a cross-disciplinary and integrative focus. Through the work of the Center, we attempt to model this approach.

The Center is currently focusing on restructuring teacher education to reflect the integrative nature of learning and teaching. It has pursued and received grants for this purpose from the California State University system and the California Department of Education.

The reader will find that this monograph contains the current and emerging thinking of nine Center members. We invite your comments and interactions as work in this area continues.

Billie Goode Blair, Ph.D.
Renate Nummela Caine, Ph.D.
Editors

What is integrative learning and teaching? How do we understand a non-fragmented reality? How do we begin to see that life and learning are more related to process and emergent events than to outcomes and objectives? This paper summarizes some of the new directions in the sciences and indicates that these have strong implications for re-conceptualizing education. The author suggests that our adherence to the Cartesian-Newtonian paradigm which emphasizes fragmentation and an illusion of static outcomes is deeply embedded in language and pedagogy. He further states that we need to articulate the language of the new sciences which is at home with terms like complexity, emergence, holism, unpredictability, disequilibrium and teleology, and that, as we begin to understand and define these terms for education, a new vision and type of educational practice will result.

LANDSCAPES OF CHANGE
TOWARD A NEW PARADIGM FOR EDUCATION
Sam Crowell

The purpose of this paper is two-fold: (1) to survey the scientific and intellectual landscape that provides a foundation for a paradigmatic change in education, and (2) to offer some curricular generalizations that have implications for educational practice. The first part of this paper, therefore, will be dominated by a discussion of the reconceptualized nature of reality, based in large part on new scientific descriptions of nature. The relevance of this discussion is to establish a new foundation from which reconceptualizing may take place in education. The latter portion of this paper will explore ways in which these new ways of looking at the world can inform and guide educational practice.

It is important to note that the exploration of the ideas presented here is far from complete. The transitional task of developing and applying these ideas, however, is among the most exciting intellectual journeys facing us. In the end, we may find our way back to our selves.

Attributes of Life

Paul Davies (1988) identified nine attributes that seem to characterize all living systems. These are (1) complexity, (2) self-organization, (3) uniqueness,

(4) emergence, (5) holism, (6) unpredictability, (7) openness, interconnectedness and disequilibrium, (8) evolution, and (9) teleology. These categories emerge from the vast amount of new work in biological and related sciences. Davies notes that these concepts represent a core of common language that applies not only to living systems, but extends to non-living systems as well.

> Concepts such as coherence, synchronization, macroscopic order, complexity, spontaneous organization, adaptation, growth of structure and so on are traditionally reserved for biological systems which undeniably have "a will of their own." Yet we have been applying these terms to lasers, fluids, chemical mixtures, and mechanical systems. (p. 92)

> Any particular property of living systems can also be found in non-living systems: crystals can reproduce, clouds can grow, etc. (p. 93)

This new terminology represents a marked departure from the pervasive Cartesian-Newtonian language which has structured modern thinking. Such language led to viewing our world as a fragmented collection of parts that could be ordered, predicted and controlled. The dominate analogy was the "machine" and this analogy was accompanied by the philosophical assumptions of dualism, mechanisms and reductionism. The conceptual terminology offered by Davies is some evidence that we have moved beyond the restrictive notions formalized by Descartes and Newton. This new terminology suggests a new world of ideas that may have as significant an impact on how we think and how we live out our lives as did the ideas that preceded them.

Complexity

The universe abounds in a complex array of relationships and interrelationships that much of traditional science either ignored or explained away. The task of understanding these relationships in terms of the patterns and processes they represent involves a very different kind of science.

Traditional questions that dealt with order and symmetry used "linear" models of investigation. "Linear" systems refer to systems in which cause and effect are apparent and are related in proportionate fashion mathematically. The realization, however, that most of the world is a combination of regularity and irregularity, has made linear models no longer applicable to questions that deal with complexity. Complex structures such as coastlines, forests, mountain chains, ice sheets, and star clusters require "non-linear" models which go beyond cause-effect ideas about nature. Complexity entails the dynamic interactions that comprise the rich variety of matter. Davies observes that "complexity is hierarchical, ranging from the elaborate structure and activity of macromolecules such as proteins and nucleic acid to the exquisitely orchestrated complexity of animal behavior" (p. 94).

Organization

The variety of form and the rich network of interactions that comprise living systems display an ordered unity. "The complexity is organized and harmonized so that the organism functions as an integrated whole" (p. 94). There is an orderliness that characterizes the diversity of form and function.

Uniqueness

Living organisms, their histories, their relationships, and their evolution are unique. There are similarities that allow us to classify and identify, yet there are always specific differences. Diversity and variety are natural to life and this constitutes part of what it means to be a living organism.

Emergence

As organisms reach new levels of complexity, new and unexpected qualities emerge that cannot be explained in cause-effect terms. They are examples of novelty and seem to confirm the diction that "the whole is greater than the sum of its parts."

Holism

Living nature is characterized by its integrated form and function. Despite the sometimes large variety of constituent parts, an organism has coherence and organization that allows it to be identified.

Unpredictability

Organisms, and even the biosphere, resist detailed predictions. According to Davies, "organisms seem to possess that intriguing 'will of their own'" (p. 95). The novel and unexpected are a part of nature. For example, "cows, ants, and geraniums were in no sense inevitable products of evolution" (p. 95). Measurable predictability which many non-scientists consider to be the basis of science is not a part of non-linear systems. Though many processes appear to be automatic, we cannot predict a future state of a biological system. This applies to micro and macro phenomena.

Openness, Interconnectedness and Disequilibrium

Open systems respond dynamically to and with their environment. Openness suggests interaction and mutually interdependent relationships. There is also constant disequilibrium in nature. This represents the view of nature as dynamic movement rather than static structure. All of life is meaningful only within the context of the rest of the environment.

Evolution

Life has the ability to develop new structures and functions. Through the transmission of genetic information, through "chosen" interactions and adaptation, and through unplanned genetic changes, life seemingly participates in its own development.

Teleology

"Organisms develop and behave in an ordered and purposive way . . ." (p. 95). There is a presumed orderliness that gives direction to the life events of living organisms.

If the dominant metaphor of the Cartesian-Newtonian paradigm was the "universe as machine," perhaps a dominant metaphor of the post-Newtonian paradigm is the "universe as a living system." It is a view of the world that rejects the dominance of reductionism.

> Complete reductionism is nothing more than a vague promise founded on the outdated and now discredited concept of determinism. By ignoring the significance of higher levels in nature complete reductionism simply dodges many of the questions about the world that are most interesting . . . (Davies, 1988, p. 140)

Instead, the post-Newtonian paradigm highlights internal processes and dynamic interactions. This "self-organization" is a radical departure from an externally driven universe. From the ecological perspective of biology to the paradoxes of quantum events, the distinction between the internal and external world becomes blurred.

> As more and more attention is devoted to the study of self-organization and complexity in nature, so it is becoming clear that there must be new general principles which have yet to be discovered. We seem to be on the verge of discovering not only wholly new laws of nature, but ways of thinking about nature that depart radically from traditional science. (Davies, 1988, p. 142)

As the attributes of a post-Newtonian paradigm move from the laboratory to our consciousness, these changing assumptions provide new challenges and new questions. Three questions which pose problems which begin to define a new paradigm are (1) What is a non-fragmented reality? (2) How do we describe a world of events? and (3) What is the nature of the mind/brain connection?

What is a Non-Fragmented Reality?

The effort to understand and to explain a non-fragmented reality is a departure from traditional scientific inquiry. Much of the history of the scientific insights that have guided our thinking has dwelled on the fragmentary nature of the world. David Bohm (1980), an eminent research and theoretical physicist, argues that fragmentation is only a reality of a particular world view, based upon scientific theories that have been superceded. He insists that the new theoretical insights of science describe a different world from the fragmentary one we know.

> The prevailing tendency in science to think and perceive in terms of a fragmentary self-world view is part of a larger movement that has been developing over the ages and that pervades almost the whole of our society today . . . it gives men a picture of the whole world as constituted of nothing but an aggregate of separately existent "atomic building blocks," and provides experimental evidence . . . that this view is necessary and inevitable. In this way, people are led to feel that fragmentation is nothing but an expression of "the way everything really is" and that anything else is impossible. (p. 15)

Bohm explains that it is inevitable that persons who view the world in this way cannot but continue to perpetuate it. There will be little disposition to consider other views of reality. Moreover, he sees the implications in virtually every aspect of life. Fragmentation is a focusing upon differences and similarities to the extent that we become confused about everything. He thus concludes that because of this, a wide range of crises develop. The individual and society as a whole are dealing with social, political, economic, ecological, psychological, and other issues from a fragmentary perspective of reality based on certain notions of the universe. To view the world in a non-fragmented way requires a new way of looking at things. According to Bohm, this means "the unbroken wholeness of the totality of existence as an undivided flowing movement without border" (p. 172).

Bohm likens unbroken wholeness to the idea of a hologram (pp. 143-147). A hologram offers a three dimensional picture of an object and the entire picture is "enfolded within each region of the photographic record" (p. 177). In other words, if one were to break a tiny piece of the picture off, the tiny piece would itself be a complete hologram of the original picture. There is not a separate piece of localized matter in space and time, but rather there exists within each part the constituted whole. Bohm uses the term "holomovement" to illustrate the constant motion of all matter This new kind of order is what Bohm calls "implicate order," that which is enfolded into everything (p. 177).

Bohm believes that a non-fragmented reality is one that permits distinct "objects" to be observed as separate and as subject to particular laws of nature, but these "objects" are enfolded in the inseparable unity of the universe. His provocative explanation of wholeness attempts to direct attention to our perceptions of fragmentation and the necessity to perceive with a different "eye" a unity that is not apparent to our senses.

Another way of viewing a non-fragmented reality is to perceive the world as organized systems which constantly interact with each other within an inter-connected environment. The theoretical biologist, Ludwig von Bertalanffy, was an early voice of this point of view. As the founder of General System Theory, Bertalanffy (1975) drew his inspiration from an organismic conception of biology "which was essentially based on our understanding organisms as organized things" (p. 41). Open systems are characterized by a constant interchange with the environment. Bertalanffy gives the example that the total protein content of the human body is exchanged about every hundred days

(p. 44). He emphasizes the dynamic quality of organisms and their constant interaction. An open system is in constant disequilibrium and varying states of change. And, every change of one system has effects on others. This high degree of interaction presupposes a basic organizational unity.

Erich Jantsch synthesized Bertalanffy's ideas with those of Ilya Prigogine, a Nobel laureate in chemistry. Jantsch developed a non-fragmented view of the evolutionary process which he called "co-evolution." The principle of co-evolution states that "the development of structures in what is called microevolution mirrors the development of structures in macroevolution and vice versa. Microstructures and macrostructures evolve together as a whole" (Briggs & Peat, 1984, p. 193). "Micro" and "macro" here refer to sub-systems and systems. For example, a molecule would be a sub-system of a cell; an organism would be a sub-system of a species; and a phylum would be a sub-system of an ecosystem. Changes in micro levels and shifts at macro levels are the result of complex response systems that interact almost simultaneously (p. 194). Co-evolution embodies a non-fragmented reality that highlights the underlying unity of the natural world.

> This is the meaning of co-evolution. A structure doesn't appear in isolation either on the macro or micro level but is a phenomenon born out of an environment in which everything affects everything, like Bohm's holomovement. Co-evolution is a description of a holistic unfolding, not an interaction of separate parts. (p. 196)

Thus, from the perspectives of Bohm, Bertalanffy, Jantsch, and others, the separateness we may observe with our senses is an illusion. One that was reinforced by the Cartesian-Newtonian paradigm and one that threatens to veil the unifying connections all around us. Only as we begin to think differently about the nature of reality will we be able to investigate its challenges and insights.

How Can We Describe a World of Events?

Henry Stapp (1990), a physicist speaking on the nature of reality, stated that "basic realities are not things, but acts." Discussing this in relation to quantum mechanics, he explained that when we perceive a triangle, we are experiencing the activity of adjacency relationships rather than an actual structure. He argues for an "action ontology" that represents Heisenberg's notion to tendencies for the "actual event."

Stapp asserts that to understand quantum reality we "must undo Descartes." We must come to understand our world in terms of the processes, relationships and the "felt experience" of actual events. Making a radical departure from the traditional epistemology, Stapp sees the "mental world" as the real epistemology. There is a relationship between our experience and the actual events of the natural world.

This description of the world is one that views reality as a process of events. The world is in the process of "becoming," of being created and re-formed during each moment in time. The post-Newtonian paradigm concentrates on understanding, ordering, and participating in the processes of nature rather than viewing static structures as objective facts, to be manipulated, exploited, or controlled.

Philosophically, the process of becoming is articulated by Alfred North Whitehead in his monumental work, *Process and Reality* (1978). Here, Whitehead defines "becoming" as the "transformation of incoherence into coherence" (p. 25). He later elaborates by explaining that

> Each actual entity is a cell with atomic unity. But in analysis it can only be understood as a process; it can only be felt as a process, that is to say, as in passage. The actual entity is divisible; but is in fact undivided. The divisibility can thus only refer to it objectifications in which it transcends itself. But such transcendence is self-revelation. (p. 227)

Integration is, in fact, a process that seemingly occurs from "within" and is never really complete. The coherence of events refers to the ordering of roles and functions within a non-static, dynamic reality. We are challenged to formulate new descriptions of reality, in which the world of events is integrated with human existence.

The "truth" of human existence is inescapably bound within processes and events. Defying a static reality, this new view of the world searches for language and concepts that somehow make this understandable. Perhaps Merleau-Ponty (in Prigogine & Stengers, 1984) describes the circumstances best:

> So long as I keep before me the ideal of an absolute observer, of knowledge in the absence of any viewpoint, I can only see my situation as being a source of error. But once I have acknowledged that through it I am geared to all actions and all knowledge that are meaningful to me, and that it is gradually filled with everything that may be for me then my contract with the social in the finitude of my situation is revealed to me as the starting point of all truth, including that of science and, since we are inside truth and cannot get outside it, all that I can do is define a truth within the situation. (p. 249)

The situation finds us bound by our own existence, caught in the objective/subjective dilemma—unless that dilemma can be transcended.

What is the Nature of the Brain and Consciousness?

One of the most difficult problems in science is the connection between brain and consciousness. It is sometimes referred to as the "mind-body problem" (Davies, p. 190) or the "mind-brain connection" (Stapp, 1990). Davies gives the following explanation of the problem:

> On the one hand, neural activity in the brain is supposed to be determined by the laws of physics, as is the case with any electrical network. On the other hand, direct experience encourages us to believe that, at least in the case of intended action, that action is caused by our mental states. How can one set of events have two causes? (p. 190)

Reductive science offers no clues to this question, for it must, of necessity, deny that mental events exist. If that is done, however, the self-reference of the reductionist must also be denied, setting up an untenable argument. To accept an existence of a "self" is to affirm the existence of mental events.

Sir John Eccles (1990) suggests that the mind converts brain action into experience. He argues for the physical existence of mind in terms of quantum processes. The brain processes the physical information of the world. According to Eccles, there is only information. It is the "mind" that creates meaning from the information. The mind converts brain action into experience.

This effort to understand experience as self-created through mind leads to deeper questions regarding individual and group consciousness. For, if, as Eccles points out, "redness" is in the mind, then how do common experiences of "redness" take place?

David Bohm may offer a way out of this dilemma. For Bohm, both the observer and the observed are parts of the same indivisible process. He draws this conclusion from quantum theory which "implies that elements that are separated in space are generally non-causally and non-locally related projections of a higher-dimensional reality . . ." (p. 211). He sees consciousness as being somehow connected to the implicate order. In other words, "objective" reality is an expression of the implicate order. Consciousness, then, may be conceived of in terms of "holomovement which connects not only mind and brain but mind and matter as well." Just as the vast "sea" of energy in space is present to our perception as a sense of emptiness or nothingness so the vast "unconscious" background of explicit consciousness with all its implication is present in a similar way" (p. 210).

The universe being described is based upon very different assumptions than the world view of Descartes and Newton. As the post-Newtonian paradigm finds greater articulation in terms of its assumptions, questions, values, and methodology, new possibilities will emerge. It is clearly a period of transition, where conclusions are stated in question marks; where hope replaces certainty. It may represent for a scientific culture, a search for identity, in which we become aware that beliefs have been shattered without clear replacements. The word is out that science has been changed. But the question of new assumptions and their implications must yet be addressed.

In education, as in the rest of the culture, our practice is driven by assumptions about our world. We call this a world view. If we perceive content to be some "thing" to be learned, then we will approach instruction in a way we think will best accomplish that goal. If we think that our world is divided into objects that are basically unconnected, then we will tend to divide our curriculum into subjects, topics and unrelated categories. Moreover, we will project sensitivities that reflect separateness. If we perceive the world to be comprised of causally determined and predictable actions, then our approach toward that world will focus on behavioral management and the tendency to reduce subject matter into discrete, linear units and skills. If, on the other hand, we view content as events, if we perceive our world as connected in funda-mental ways, if we view action as self-generated within a particular context, then our curricular and instructional decisions may be very different.

The task for educators requires an openness to completely reconsider the "whats," the "whys," and the "hows" that currently dominate our thinking and practice. We also must question the institutional structures which organize and control our activities. As educators, our intellectual inquiry meets the social world "head-on." Donald Oliver (1989) discusses the task of translating these ideas within a cultural context.

> [T]he major challenge in working toward a new and positive conception of culture is not the discounting or casting out of some quality of feeling or understanding, but rather the inclusion of aspects of universe/nature which have tended to be under-appreciated. The problem is finding ways of reconstruing and experiencing the world with greater balance, fullness, interrelated-ness. Such integration would include breaking down the barriers

> between the functional specializations that segregate our consciousness. . . . Integration includes the deliberate search for occasions in which ontological understanding informs and relates to technical knowing. It includes activities that enrich a broad range of metaphorical sensibilities. In Sorokian terms, it means creating a culture and an education in which there is some balance among various modes of satisfaction, where mind, body, and spirit are not reified as separate qualities of being to be expressed and appreciated in separate times and ways and places. (p. 29)

Oliver hopes that new visions of culture will include "qualities of becoming, qualities of being, qualities of knowing; qualities of participation and connection" (p. 55). In the following section we will explore the implications of an educational practice based upon these new assumptions of reality.

A New Foundation for Education

Joseph Campbell (1986) writes "The old gods are dead or dying and people everywhere are searching, asking: What is the new mythology to be, the mythology of this unified earth as of one harmonious being?" (p. 17). Certainly in education the desire to know and to understand so that we may instruct others is deeply felt by many. There is an innate sense that "real knowledge" is just beyond our grasp. Yet, Campbell goes on to say

> One cannot predict the next mythology any more than one can predict tonight's dream; for a mythology is not an ideology. It is not something projected from the brain, but something experienced from the heart, from recognitions of identities behind or within the appearances of nature, perceiving with love a "thou" where there would have been otherwise only an "it." (p. 17)

Part of what these new assumptions suggest is that there is not a new set of information that suddenly replaces the old. Knowledge is perceived within experience and cannot be separated from the personal meaning given to it by the individual. Knowledge without any relationship to meaning is what Whitehead calls "inert knowledge"; there is little possibility of it making a difference.

To be serious in our attempt to understand a new paradigm is to participate in its development. As William Doll (1988) points out, we must be "willing to face an uncertain future uncertainly; that is without confidence in absolute standards" (p. 16). Doll writes of the need to change our view of curriculum from its emphasis on a "course-to-be-run" to the "running-of-the-course."

> This is not . . . to argue for the relativism which permeated both progressive and open education. Rather, this is to say that the world we live in is both complex and emergent. As complex it has disorder and chaos built into its very nature. . . . As emergent, our world or universe is not pre-set, predictable, discoverable. It is continually coming into being, in part through our interactions with the environment, our "dialogues with nature . . ." (pp. 16-17)

Hence, approaching the development of a new paradigm, one should not expect a final product. It is an on-going process through which we learn "to look at ourselves looking at the world." Below are offered five ways of "viewing" educational practice which build upon the previous discussion.

Complexity

Complexity is everywhere in educational practice! The reality of the classroom is that it is multilayered, without a beginning or an end. Students affect each other, the teacher, what is taught, how it is taught and any outcomes that might occur. This is true on an individual basis as well as in a collective sense. There is a dynamic nature about the classroom to which a teacher constantly responds. The teacher is continually trying to understand and monitor the complexity and make sense of it. Everything is affecting everything. The thoughts, feelings, attitudes and dispositions of each individual are interacting with rapidity to a potentially infinite number of stimuli. Yet each "class" also has its own personality, as well. Understanding this complexity in terms of an open, non-linear system lets us see this complexity as a natural part of life and as a set of relationships which offer immense possibilities.

Complexity consists of relationships and interrelationships. Where do these exist in the classroom? Where do these exist in curricula and subject matter? In what ways are we interconnected by function and purpose? These questions allow us to experience each other in a different way, to build upon multiple perspectives and multiple abilities, and to understand content in terms of relationships and patterns. Understanding subject matter in this way opens up whole new possibilities of "content."

Complexity is interactive. There is an open, playful approach to ideas, especially as these ideas emerge from our experience. Paulo Freire (1983) writes of "dialogical" education in which students and teachers are engaged in a "pedagogical situation"; a communication of lived experience in relation to a particular issue. Vygotsky (1978) notes the importance of "social reciprocity" and the human ability to learn from others. Interactive approaches to instruction offer opportunities to reduce the isolation of the learner's experience. Viewing educational practice as complexity and resisting the temptation to "reduce" this complexity and, instead, to take advantage of it, is a challenge ahead of us.

Self-Organization

Self-organization in education implies that each individual learner is continually "ordering" or "making sense of" their experience. As new experiences and information are dealt with, the learner assimilates them with previously-ordered experience. In other words, we create meaning for ourselves constantly. Caine and Caine (1991) describe this process in terms of brain functioning. "In a sense the brain is both artist and scientist, attempting to discern and understand patterns as they occur, and giving expression to unique and creative patterns of its own." Bruner (1986) suggests that humans have the remarkable ability to go beyond particular information and to create new forms of knowledge. Piaget's notion of "autoregulation" describes the transformative process of learning. Learners "order" their environment.

There is an emergent quality also in self-organization. Inherent in the assumption is that "novelty" is generated through this ordering of experience. This generative aspect of learning suggests that instructional approaches that encourage this to take place may have great promise. An example of such an approach is the use of metaphor in teaching. Students generate with the teacher new metaphorical insights which may then be "unpacked" and reordered. As Lakoff and Johnson (1980) suggest, metaphors are central to our thinking process and abound throughout our language. Rather than being merely a linguistic technique, metaphors play a central role in both our understanding and expression of the world. Generative approaches to learning offer new ways to mediate our experience. The nature of educational practice changes when we build upon the self-organizational abilities of students.

Process

There are no static realities; there are only events in process. This assumption challenges our sense perception perhaps more than any other. A rock, for example, is not a static "thing." It is a unified collection of millions of micro-events. It is also an on-going collection of histories, functions, and relationships. Viewing matter and concepts in this way necessarily changes the questions we ask and the information we provide. It allows us to participate in a celebration of life. When learning becomes a celebration of significant occasions it opens us to creative expressions that convey meaning as well as content. The use of art, drama, dance, music, and literature to celebrate the processes at work in all of life creates a different kind of curriculum. On one hand the "objective" information is not excluded and on the other hand, the significance of the processes inherent in nature is experienced expressively.

"Process" in curriculum has traditionally meant the process of inquiry. Usually this has meant skills. Proponents have dichotomized the issue by presenting it as Content vs. Process. New paradigmatic assumptions however do not suggest that one is more important than the other; nor would it even be appropriate to say that both content and process are important. What these new assumptions suggest is that content and process are inseparable and to divide them is to fragment our new understanding of reality. This view demands that we reconceptualize the debate and understand that content *is* process and vice versa. As participant observers we are inescapably connected to what is studied. We cannot study a "rock" without studying ourselves.

Since we are connected to what we are experiencing and learning, it follows naturally that reflecting upon the learning experience, itself, our feelings about the experience and projected extensions is an important part of curriculum. Caine and Caine (1991) tell us that all learning is physiological. Learning involves previous experience, emotions, personal and social goals, and attitudinal predispositions. Learners approach thinking and the connecting of experience differently. All of this provides enormous possibilities for both curriculum and instruction. The Caines call this "active processing." Active processing is "the consolidation and internalization of information, by the learner, in a way that is personally meaningful and conceptually coherent" (p. 206). The process of learning, thinking, feeling provides a broader and deeper perspective of our role as educators.

Unity

In 1854, Chief Seattle composed a letter to President Franklin Pierce responding to a request to sell land to the United States government. His letter expresses an understanding of unity that we today can only barely approach.

> How can you buy or sell the sky, the warmth of the land?
> The idea is strange to us.

> If we do not own the freshness of the air and the sparkle of the water, how can you buy them?
>
> Every part of this earth is sacred to my people. Every shining pine needle, every sandy shore, every mist in the dark woods, every clearing and humming insect is holy in the memory and experience of my people. The sap which courses through the trees carries the memories of the red man.

Chief Seattle expresses the understanding that we, our histories, and our experiences are not separated from the world around us. They are, inevitably, a part of who we are and who we may become. He writes that "All things are connected," and that "Man did not weave the web of life; he is merely a strand in it. Whatever he does to the web, he does to himself."

Unity assumes that there is some fundamental connectedness. In addition, an awareness of this connectedness brings a sense of meaning and purposefulness. It is this underlying significance that we should strive to bring alive in curriculum. Just as Bohm's implicate order suggests that underneath the explicate nature we perceive a unified sense of meaning, so in curriculum, inherent in all content is an opportunity to become more aware of ourselves, our connectedness with the rest of nature, and our participation in the processes of life.

Donald Oliver (1989) shares an example of first graders who were given a simple story about planting a pumpkin seed. They were asked to sequence the order of events. Such an activity is an example of "technical" knowing in which emphasis is placed on a particular skill. He notes

> The child is not encouraged to hold a pumpkin, to feel a pumpkin, to feel *like* a pumpkin. There is no effort to present the mystery of birth and life and death and rebirth involved . . . in the story. The story could be a drama; it could be visual; it could have smell and taste. It could be a dance. (pp. 183-184)

Oliver also shows how these expressive activities could be expanded into a discussion of such questions as "Are humans 'rooted' in any way similar to plants? Are humans 'freer' than plants? Do plants communicate when they respond to sunlight and moisture? Does the plant feel loved when it is taken care of—as does a human baby?" (p. 185). Such experiences and questions create an intimate relationship with that which is being studied. It is this kind of experience that helps learners feel connected to the world being studied. And it does not preclude being able to sequentially order sentences!

Context

Events and occasions occur within an environment, within a situational moment. That "situation" cannot be separated from the experience. The "situation" is both internal and external at the same time. Educators for a long time have noted the importance of the environment. The environment, however, has been viewed as something external to the learner, something to manipulate and control in order to achieve a particular "desirable" outcome. The assumptions of a post-Newtonian paradigm reject this deterministic outlook. The context of a situation is always a part of the situation itself.

Caine and Caine (1991) write of creating a context for learning through what they call "orchestrated immersion." This refers to the establishment of "powerfully evocative, challenging, meaningful and coherent environments . . ." (p. 149). Learners, when exposed to these settings, are able to integrate their experiences as well as to extend them to new or novel situations. The ability to create moods, themes, dialogues, and activities which accentuate learning becomes a new requirement for teachers. Blending practice with reflection, expression with inquiry, and performance with command, the teacher becomes an artist. Mastery is not marked by self-indulgence or cumulative skills, but rather by service and accomplishment. As learners become immersed in a context of significant occasions the internal and the external become one.

Context includes the organizational environment in which learning takes place. Schools must be reconceptualized to become learning organizations. Such organizations create opportunities for interaction and create a sense of dynamic unity. There is an ever-evolving purpose that is built upon and recreated daily. Mechanistic operations are de-emphasized. School becomes more than a place, it becomes a concept of support and integration. It becomes a community of nourishment and transformation.

Conclusion

This paper has summarized some of the important directions of twentieth century science that form a foundation for new ways of viewing our world. These insights provide new opportunities to transform our thinking and practice. As we begin to search for educational applications, we must always be cautious to claim too much. Yet, education has been mired for too long in a mechanized practice that fragments our world and directs us away from an integrated reality. As our questions change, so will our answers. It is my hope that we can legitimize the asking of new questions.

Not addressed directly in this paper is the changing face of educational research. A changing "landscape" requires new maps. It may also require new map-making processes. What comes across over and over again in studying these ideas is that metaphorically, the map-makers are part of the landscape being mapped. This requires that we are constantly looking inward at the same time we look outward. This above all else holds the promise for transformation.

John Briggs and David Peat (1984) comment on the work of scientists who have made wholeness a part of theoretical science.

> They have shown how wholeness may be infused in every part and particle of our lives. We will not endeavor to predict what acknowledging such a universe could mean for the whole conduct of human affairs, since it is possible such recognition could transform human consciousness itself.
> For thousands of years wholeness has been mute. Now it can speak. Who can tell what it will say? (p. 271)

May we be one of the voices of "wholeness."

References

Bertalanffy, L. (1975). *Perspectives on general system theory.* New York: George Braziller.

Bohm, D. (1980). *Wholeness and the implicate order.* London: Routledge and Kegan Paul.

Briggs, J., & Peat, F. D. (1984). *Looking glass universe: The emerging science of wholeness.* New York: Simon and Schuster.

Bruner, Jerone S. (1986). *Actual minds, possible worlds.* Cambridge, MA: Harvard University Press.

Caine, R. N., & Caine G. (1991). *Making connections: Teaching and the human brain.* Virginia: ASCD.

Campbell, J. (1986). *The inner reaches of outer space.* New York: Harper and Row.

Davies, P. (1988). *The cosmic blueprint: New discoveries in nature's ability to order the universe.* New York: Simon and Schuster.

Doll, W. (1988). *A post-modern view of curriculum.* Monograph for Louisiana State University.

Eccles, J. (1990, February). Presentation at the Conference for the Study of Human Consciousness, San Francisco.

Freire, Paulo (1983). *Pedagogy of the oppressed.* New York: Continuum.

Lakoff, G., & Johnson, M. (1980). *Metaphors we live by.* Chicago: The University of Chicago Press.

Oliver, D. (1989). *Education, modernity, and fractured meaning.* Albany, NY: State University of New York Press.

Prigogine, I., & Stengers, I. (1984). *Order out of chaos: Man's new dialogue with nature.* New York: Bantam Books.

Stapp, H. (1990, February). Presentation at the Conference for the Study of Human Consciousness, San Francisco.

Whitehead, A. N. (1978). *Process and reality.* New York: Free Press.

Vygotsky, L. S. (1978). *Mind in society: The development of higher psychological processes.* Cambridge, MA: Harvard University Press.

Teaching Jimmy to fly a kite may involve some direct instruction, but anyone who ever experienced flying a kite on the beach will recall that they also learned about the feeling of sand under bare feet, the smell and sound of the sea, the feel of the wind as it pulled on the string, and at the same time managed spontaneously complex mathematical calculations of distance and speed. Additionally they developed an attitude about flying kites, either pursued or abandoned the sport, and possibly learned something about parents' patience and so on.

The notion of integrative learning presupposes that learning always occurs at complex psycho/physiological and emotional levels. In this paper Caine and Caine provide us with a set of principles from the neurosciences which re-vision the learner as one engaged in multiple levels when learning. The implications are that the best learning occurs when learners are immersed in orchestrated, complex, meaningful experiences.

THE USE OF BRAIN RESEARCH AS A
BASIS FOR EVALUATING INTEGRATIVE
APPROACHES TO EDUCATION
Renate Nummela Caine
and Geoffrey Caine

As the crisis in education deepens, educators are beginning to search for alternative approaches to traditional modes of instruction. Some of the alternatives include more complex, integrative methodologies such as suggestopedia, brain compatible learning, whole language, Optimalearning, accelerative learning, learning styles and thematic instruction. What we are missing at this point is a unifying theory of learning which helps us to assess the claims of the different approaches, explains when and why integrative models work, and offers some guidelines for "cross-fertilization" among methods.

We believe, after sorting through several models of brain functioning and many research findings, that the current available research on the brain provides us with the insights and direction we need. We have examined the "left-brain right-brain" research (Springer and Deutsch, 1985), MacLean's theory of the triune brain (Nummela and Rosengren, 1986), research into brain plasticity (Diamond, 1987), models of memory (O'Keefe and Nadel, 1978) among others.

Of course, the topic is enormously complex and there is still much debate among neuroscientists. However, it is possible to take some fundamental conclusions from the brain research and translate these into basic set of assumptions about the human learner and learning.

When this is done, we become aware of the fact that learners are much more complex than traditional approaches to learning and teaching have led us to believe. We also begin to appreciate the role that innovative and integrative approaches play in expanding our notion of teaching. What follows is that we begin to make available a guide for educators which can help them understand, select from and apply the various alternative and traditional methodologies.

Our conclusions take the form of a set of twelve principles (Caine and Caine, 1990, 1991) which take us far beyond brain dominance theory into a neurologically sound foundation for teaching and learning. We have sought to "field test" these in several ways. One approach has been to make presentations to a wide variety of audiences for the purpose of eliciting comment and discussion. For example, the principles were presented in May 1989 at the National Conference of the American Society for Training and Development, in September 1989 at the National Conference of the International Society for Exploring Teaching Alternatives, and in October 1989 at the North American division of the World Conference on Education for All, sponsored by several United Nations agencies as well as other organizations.

With these principles as a foundation, we have also sought to identify a set of essential characteristics that must be present for learning to be regarded as genuinely based on what we know about the brain (Caine and Caine, 1990, 1991 in press). Our objective here is to summarize the principles and to indicate some of the essential ingredients of integrative learning methodologies.

Principals for Brain-Based Learning

We begin by quoting liberally from our writing (Caine and Caine, 1990, 1991) referred to above:

Principle One: The brain is a parallel processor. The brain ceaselessly performs many functions simultaneously. Thoughts, emotions, imagination and predispositions operate concurrently and interact with other brain processes involving health maintenance and the expansion of knowledge. *Education needs to embrace and deal with all the dimensions of parallel processing.*

Principle Two: Learning engages the entire physiology. The brain functions according to physiological rules. Learning is as natural as breathing, and it is possible to cither inhibit or facilitate it. In fact, the actual "wiring" of the brain is affected by our life and educational experiences. *Anything that affects our physiological functioning affects our capacity to learn.*

Principle Three: The search for meaning is innate. The search for meaning (making sense of our experiences) is survival-oriented and basic to the human brain. The brain needs and automatically registers the familiar while simultaneously searching for and responding to novel stimuli. *Hence, both familiarity and novelty must be combined in a learning environment.*

Principle Four: The search for meaning occurs through "patterning." In a way, the brain is both scientist and artist, attempting to discern and understand patterns as they occur and giving expression to unique and creative patterns of its own. The brain resists having meaninglessness imposed on it. By meaninglessness we mean isolated pieces of information unrelated to what makes sense to a particular learner. *Really effective education must give learners an opportunity to formulate their own patterns of understanding. That means they need an opportunity to put skills and ideas together in their own way.*

Principle Five: Emotions are critical to patterning. What we learn is influenced and organized by emotions and mind-sets involving expectancy, personal biases and prejudices, self-esteem and the need for social-interaction.

Emotions and thoughts literally shape each other and cannot be separated. Moreover, the emotional impact of any lesson or life experience may continue to reverberate long after the specific event that triggers it. *Hence an appropriate emotional climate is indispensable to sound education.*

Principle Six: Every brain simultaneously perceives and creates parts and wholes. Although there is some truth to the "left-brain right-brain" distinction, that is not the whole story. In a healthy person, both hemispheres interact in every activity, from art and computing to sales and accounting. The "two brain" doctrine is most useful for reminding us that the brain reduces information into parts and perceives holistically at the same time. *Good training and education recognizes this, for instance, by introducing global projects and ideas from the very beginning.*

Principle Seven: Learning involves both focused attention and peripheral perception. The brain absorbs information of which it is directly aware, but it also directly absorbs information that lies beyond the immediate focus of attention. In fact it responds to the entire sensory context in which teaching and communication occur. These "peripheral signals" are extremely potent. Even the unconscious signals that reveal inner attitudes and beliefs have a powerful impact on students. *Educators, therefore, can and should pay extensive attention to all facets of the educational environment.*

Principle Eight: Learning always involves conscious and unconscious processes. Much of our learning is the result of unconscious processing. Moreover it is the entire experience that is processed. That means that much understanding may NOT occur during a class, but may occur hours, weeks or months later. It also means that educators must design what they do so as to facilitate subsequent unconscious processing of experience by students. *In practice, this includes proper design of the context, the incorporation of reflection and metacognitive activities and ways to help learners creatively elaborate on the content of a course.*

Principle Nine: We have at least two types of memory. A spatial/ autobiographical memory system and a set of systems for rote learning. We have a natural spatial memory which does not need rehearsal and allows for "instant" memory of experiences. This is the system that registers the details of your meal last night. It is always engaged, is inexhaustible and is motivated by novelty. We also have a set of systems for recalling relatively unrelated information. They are motivated by reward and punishment. Thus meaningful and meaningless information is organized and stored differently. *The only way for people to deal effectively with vast amounts of new information and regular retraining is to learn for meaning.*

Principle Ten: The brain understands and remembers best when facts and skills are embedded in natural spatial memory. Our native language is learned through multiple, interactive experiences. It is shaped by internal processes and by social interaction. In fact, any complex subject is given meaning when embedded in real experience. *The point is that appropriate experiences are more complex than have traditionally been thought. They go far beyond simulation or role playing, and include such things as the real relationships, the real context and the real projects that are actually involved.*

Principle Eleven: Learning is enhanced by challenge and inhibited by threat. The brain learns best when it makes maximum connections and optimally when appropriately challenged, but it "downshifts" under perceived threat. Under these conditions, it becomes less flexible and reverts to primitive attitudes and procedures. That is why we must create and maintain an atmosphere of relaxed alertness, involving low threat and high challenge. Moreover, that needs to be the state of mind of the instructor, as well. However, low threat is NOT synonymous with simply "feeling good." The essential element of a perceived threat is a feeling of *helplessness.* Occasional stress and anxiety are inevitable and are to be expected in genuine learning. The reason is that deep level changes lead to a reorganization of the self and that can be intrinsically stressful, irrespective of the skill of, and support offered by, a teacher. *What learners need to acquire, above all, is a belief in their capacity to change and learn.*

Principle Twelve: Every brain is unique. We all have the same set of systems, and yet all are different. *That is why choice, variety and multi-sensory processes are essential.*

Implications

Many of us are familiar with some of these principles but have primarily dealt with them as separate and discrete factors that can affect learning. We may not have seen them as operating together. Yet all of these principles are operating simultaneously in every learner. When that complexity is properly understood, we are looking at a very different way to approach the teaching/learning process. There are at least three major implications:

a. The principles show that ALL learning is experiential! Irrespective of what we seek to teach or learn, all the brain/mind systems are engaged, every feature of the context is having an impact and the brain is constantly seeking to make sense of, or dismiss, all that it experiences, whether the instructor is aware of those facts or not. What a student learns depends upon the real life, moment-to-moment set of experiences and contexts in which the training or education is embedded. Content is not separate from context—environment is not separate from creative thought—transfer of training is dependent upon environment and so on.

Given the ongoing and total immersion of a student in life experience, one ingredient of the art of teaching becomes that of appropriately orchestrating experience. Hence art, music, thematic integration, rich social relationships and so on are indispensable. Integrating the curriculum thus becomes a natural and essential part of teaching.

What needs to be understood, however, is that the student cannot be isolated from the immensity of his or her real experience. Orchestration does not stop in the classroom. It is influenced by life. Thus, the location of a school or classroom, the embeddedness of course content in real life experience, the weather, relationships with friends, family and colleagues, health, social and business activities, sources of entertainment, exposure to the media and a host of other factors are always interacting with a student's inner life to shape the experience of content. In the end, the way in which life is incorporated into education is as important as the methods we use and the classroom experiences that we create.

b. Integrative approaches to learning calls for identifying very different types of learning outcomes—outcomes that take us beyond our reliance on memorization, to outcomes which measure meaningful learning. The distinction between the two tends to be obscured by over-specification of educational objectives. When we teach for specific and identifiable performance, such as the capacity to solve quadratic equations, we can teach for memory and succeed. That is, a student can master fairly complex skills that satisfy testing requirements and still have no in-depth understanding of what is involved in the skill or discipline.

The demonstration of genuine understanding is much more complex. It includes, for example, the capacity to spontaneously solve fairly complex but unpredictable problems in a particular domain such as computing. It also involves the learner's ability to integrate the field or subject into new and different contexts.

This distinction has a very subtle but very powerful effect. If we use complex methodologies but aim for a very simple and over-specified result, we actually inhibit the capacity of the learner to be creative and develop deeper insights (that is, to maximize connections between what is already in the brain and new meanings). Hence our methodology can become a series of tricks to aid memory. It is absolutely essential that some of our outcomes be open ended, and that teachers are NOT totally authoritative in all respects. That is the condition that gives the learner a sense of permission to develop ideas of their own.

   c. *All learning is developmental.* Among other things, learning engages the entire physiology and the entire self, and both body and psyche take time to change. People are different, and move at different speeds. Moreover there are times when long term understanding requires in-depth penetration of a subject in the short term. The cumulative implication from these and other principles is that we need to be extremely cautious about accelerating learning as an end in itself. This is so primarily because such acceleration inevitably refers to memorization of one sort or another. As the principles make clear, we need to look for teaching which allows the learner to make multiple and maximum connections between what is known and what is learned. What we are looking for is long term "mapping" in the brain. That kind of learning includes passively and actively processing what is experienced, and it takes time.

Conclusion

   Much still needs to be done for integrative methodologies to make it into the average public school classroom. In particular, it seems to us that educators must have a comprehensive and solid theory of learning. They must know why alternative methodologies work better than the traditional approaches of "symbol specific" learning. Educators need assistance in understanding what their educational objectives need to be, with particular emphasis on going beyond testing for the memorization of meaningless information. They need to understand what is happening in the classroom and in the world beyond. They need help in identifying and selecting those approaches that will be of value. And they need more tools in the social and political debate about the direction that education is to take.

   Developing a theoretical foundation is critical work. There is also a need for research that helps us to synthesize what is already known, that furthers our understanding of how to assess individual aspects of integrative learning/teaching and that helps us to define and measure outcomes which will be as diverse and complex as the learners we are teaching. We offer the brain principles in support of those endeavors.

References

Caine, R. N., & Caine, G. (1990). Understanding a brain-based approach to learning and teaching. *Educational Leadership, 48,* 66-69.

Caine, R. N., & Caine, G. (1991). *Making connections: Teaching and the human brain.* Alexandria, VA: ASCD.

Diamond, M. C. (1987, January). *Brain growth in response to experience.* Seminar, San Francisco. Paper presented at Educating Tomorrow's Children.

MacLean, P. D. (1978). A mind of three minds: Educating the triune brain. In *Seventy-seventh yearbook of the National Society for the Study of Education* (pp. 308-342). Chicago: University of Chicago Press.

MacLean, P. D. (1969). New trends in man's evolution. In *A triune concept of the brain and behavior: Papers presented at Queen's University, Ontario, 1969.* Ann Arbor, MI: Books on Demand, UMI.

Nummela, R. M., & Rosengren, T. (1986). What's happening in students' brains may redefine teaching. *Educational Leadership, 43,* 49-53.

Nummela, R., & Rosengren, T. (1988). The brain's routes and maps: Vital connections in learning. *NAASP Bulletin—The Journal for Middle Level and High School Administrators, 72,* 83-86.

O'Keefe, J., & Nadel, J. (1978). *The hippocampus as a cognitive map.* New York: Oxford University Press.

Springer, S., & Deutsch, G. (1985). *Left brain, right brain* (2nd ed.). New York: W. H. Freeman and Company.

Administrative involvement in structuring and supporting integrative learning experiences is seen as vital to the successful functioning of schools. The author suggests that administrators need skills which can ensure effective leadership of school staff in planning integrative instructional approaches. An explanatory model of planning is provided to guide administrators and staffs in the creative design of curriculum and instructional processes. The author describes the accomplishment of an integrative curriculum as requiring "planning literacy" and suggests that perceived obstacles can be overcome by adoption of planning-literate concepts.

ADMINISTRATIVE INVOLVEMENT
IN INTEGRATIVE LEARNING:
COMPREHENSIVE PLANNING PROCESSES
Billie Goode Blair

As early as 1929, Alfred North Whitehead urged the eradication of the "fatal disconnection of subjects which kills the vitality of our modern curriculum" (pp. 10-11). Many theorists since that time have proposed an *integrated* curriculum, to provide unified views of commonly held knowledge, and an *integrative* curriculum to enable learners to develop their own structures in order to make sense of the world of knowledge (Dressel, 1958; Turner, 1986; Harter and Gehrke, 1989).

The vision for an integration of the curriculum and of learning is that teachers, working across artificial boundaries such as disciplines, grade levels and age groupings, will be able to forge an engaging and effective learning process for students. This vision requires that teachers possess several attributes and commitments. Included among these requirements are: (1) *ability* to foresee the need and the function of an integrative approach; (2) *willingness* to dedicate extended hours of work to the task of integrative learning; (3) *resolution* to work as part of a team to accomplish the task; (4) *perspicacity* to design a comprehensive approach to integrating the curriculum; (5) *determination* to petition the school administrators to allow organizational changes; and (6) *fortitude and dedication* to carry the process from planning through design, implementation, and evaluation.

The question which arises is: given the critical need for integrative learning, will teachers be able to rally among themselves to gain support for an integrative approach? There are many competent teachers who serve in today's educational systems and many who regularly exhibit impressive leadership skills. However, regardless of the talent pool, the reality appears to be that most teachers are reluctant to take responsibility for initiation and implementation of integrative learning, as outlined in the steps above. Teachers interviewed on the topic are generally willing to dedicate extended hours to the task (step 2) and will resolve to work as part of a team (step 3). Teachers who have been approached to initiate other requirements, however, have expressed reluctance (Blair, 1990).

To understand teachers' reluctance requires an analysis of the organizational approach that will be required for integrative learning. In requiring coordination across disciplines and other artificial boundaries, the requirement actually is that a redesign of the organization's structure be accomplished. This situation can be understood when the nature of integrative learning is examined more specifically. For example, teachers who were once attached rigorously to disciplines or subject areas might, under an integrative learning realignment, hold lesser allegiance to these organizational facets than to the overall notion of blurred but interlocking subject areas and enhanced student interest and outcomes. To accomplish such a realignment, organizationally, will mean that a careful and comprehensive planning process must be carried out to study and, subsequently, design the realignments. Planning processes are most effective if all those at the school site are involved in the planning (Holmberg, 1979). Since administrators are charged with the responsibility for total school staffs, it seems reasonable, therefore, to encourage administrators to assume leadership roles to understand, endorse and facilitate an integrative learning realignment. Administrators who can lead their staffs through the design of a more appropriate learning process will have been able to develop a vision of the future that can be enacted through a comprehensive, or, long-range planning process.

To date, most administrators are not accomplished at carrying out planning processes—primarily, because administrators have been slow to utilize and endorse comprehensive planning. There is a tendency to believe that precise planning processes, including long-range and strategic planning, are for the profit-making sector. Education's brand of planning, it is believed, is one of response—characterized by solving immediate, daily problems, on-the-spot and as they arise. In organizational psychology and management circles, this approach is known as "crisis management." While there is no avoiding the day-to-day solution of problems, there are other approaches which can provide more control and better resolution of both daily problems and future effectiveness. Drucker (1974) describes the merits of using today's knowledge and actions as the springboard for plans of the future. He sees the long-range as made up of short-range decisions, and states that "unless decisions on the here and now are integrated into one unified [long-term] plan of action, they will be [but] expedient, guess and misdirection" (p. 122).

There are a number of reasons, therefore, why comprehensive planning processes are ignored by administrators and, consequently, why such promising practices as integrative learning do not get instituted. *One reason,* as mentioned above, is that of unfamiliarity with the planning function—never having had an opportunity to learn the how, when, where and why of planning from role models using these processes, or through formal training. *Another* is not having the resources to devote to a planning process—that is, lacking the arrangements of time and money to involve staff in formalized planning processes. And *a third* is one of time management—when the crises of today mitigate against acknowledgement of the future. Time management, of course, is also related to lack of knowledge concerning "a better way," or, the comprehensive planning function.

For whatever reasons, educational administrators continue to miss an opportunity to tap the creative expertise of themselves and their staffs for use in the enhancement of educational systems. Holmberg (1979) contends that administrators who do not involve themselves with comprehensive planning and who do not act as planners for their schools overlook a basic management function. Ignorance of planning functions or a reluctance to utilize planning processes, according to Holmberg, most often results in the loss to education of truly innovative solutions and allows others—the state, federal government, pressure groups or even a district office—to control the destiny of school site functions. Because knowledge of planning function is becoming increasingly more important, the possession and use of this knowledge can be termed a "planning literacy." Becoming "planning literate" is seen by this author as one of the greatest needs for administrators of the future. Appropriate functioning of administrators and excellence in school administration can not be insured until planning, as a process, is learned and utilized. Planning literacy, therefore, currently represents a problem for administrators. Several solutions to the problem, however, can be suggested.

Solving the Problem of Planning Literacy

Even a short course in planning is best accomplished over a period of several days. However, the basic elements of planning are presented in the discussion which follows and can be used in the absence of more formal courses in planning. The elements of planning which will be discussed in this paper are: (1) dedication, (2) exploration, (3) distillation, (4) utilization, (5) characterization, and (6) revitalization. The exploration of these elements which follows is intended to assist a potential planning-literate administrator, as well as others who will be working with the administrator, in understanding the planning process. Understanding and exemplifying each of the elements will provide a basis for initiating planning.

The Six Elements of Planning

Element One: Dedication

In any planning process, the first step is to determine that planning is needed and to understand why this is so. In other words, there is a need to be dedicated to the notion of planning. There are many factors which generate and sustain dedication. The quest for excellence in management is one factor. The desire for better use of limited funds and resources is another. And satisfaction in attainment of greater staff participation in educational goals is yet another. In the case of instituting planning for integrative learning, the desire to foster a stronger and more effective teaching force for the long term would be a factor, as well as to ensure that groups of students are no longer forgotten in the educational process. Regardless of the motivation which generates dedication, this element must be present before any other of the elements can be considered. It seems reasonable to assume that dedication to planning for integrative learning can best be inspired by the education of administrators and teachers on the topic of an integrative curriculum. The various aspects and benefits of integrative learning should be presented and explored during this educative process.

Element Two: Exploration

Once dedication has been established, the next step is to explore and assess needs. This means that a formalized approach must be used to understand both the specific needs of the constituency which the school system serves and the needs of the staff who serve the system. The best way to ensure success in assessing needs and collecting data is to obtain information from a variety of sources. Preliminary to the design of a formal needs assessment tool, a task force of citizen advisors can be asked to verbalize the needs and desires held by the community for educational preparation of its youth. Likewise, internal needs can be surfaced and clarified by asking a staff task force of advisors to designate needs inherent in their participation in the educational process. In the design of an integrative curriculum, better insight into staff and student needs will assist in greater effectiveness both of the design and of execution in the new learning situation. Data gained through needs assessments of community and staff should be supplemented by demographic data obtained from a regional association of governments, the district or county office, the State Department of Finance, and the Center for Continuing Study of the California Economy, among others.

Element Three: Distillation

Once information has been obtained during the exploration stage, the step which follows involves synthesis, review and analysis for meaning—or, discovering, in a systematic way, what the data reveal. "Distillation," therefore is the manner in which this process takes place. It is during this step that a school staff works together to look at the data, to understand it and to describe its importance. It is at this point that a formulation of mission, goals and objectives is designed to respond to expressed needs. During this process, school staffs interested in integrative learning will be able to develop some insight into possible grouping of materials and other configurations of student learning requirements. Foremost in this process is the articulation of a mission or purpose of the organization, as perceived by those involved in the organization and in response to the expressed needs of both the "consumers" (community) and the "producers" (staff).

Element Four: Utilization

Continuing the planning sequence to this stage means that, in response to the formulated plan (that is, the written philosophy, goals and objectives, from the distillation stage), a plan of action, or, utilization, must immediately follow.

This action plan is to be a carefully-crafted document which provides clear direction, task responsibility and timelines for utilizing information obtained by the planning participants and for converting that information into purposeful action. The plan of action will drive the future functioning of the site's educational system. For example, if an integrative curriculum is to be the result of the planning, the plan will provide details about subject matter coordination, themes and other organizers, teacher collaboration, grade and student configurations, expected outcomes and time-frame considerations relative to proposed changes. The action plan, as originally written, along with data on implementation and management are central foci for the "characterization" stage, which describes the fifth planning element.

Element Five: Characterization

Once the plan has been in operation for a period of time (usually six months to one year), it is necessary to determine how the system functions and, therefore, its programmatic meaning to education. This task is accomplished by comparing the *planned* system to the *actual* system. This comparison provides a "characterization" of what the organization is like, contextualized to what was intended. By collecting data on system and program function at this stage, judgments concerning operational effectiveness are possible. Effectiveness is determined by measuring originally-stated planning philosophy, goals and objectives with actual planning outcomes. Once the operating system has been characterized, a determination can be made concerning whether expectations were met and revision is needed. The sixth and final stage of the cyclical process, therefore, describes the "revitalization" element of planning.

Element Six: Revitalization

During the "characterization" stage, the nature of the operating design has been determined. That is, the process of characterization allows determination of *what* functions the system performs and *whether* these functions are in keeping with the original program intent. If it is found that system implementation (for example, the functioning of an integrative curriculum at a school site) has been faithful to original intent, then the revitalization stage will consist of future planning which extends current functions into the future. A study of the future will be necessary, at this point, to assure continuing viability of the program. The study will take into account, for example, better and even more effective ways of providing the coordination necessary for an integrative learning environment and will produce more effective means for participation of all concerned. In the worst case, if the plan is determined to be off-target regarding its original intent, the revitalization stage will consist of: (1) redesign to ensure better congruence with original intent, or (2) redesign of the original philosophy and goals for greater congruence with the present operation. For example, it might be determined through study during the utilization stage that integrative learning was not well understood when the project was begun, but, after a year's work, the acquired meaning will allow an improved planning design for the following year's implementation. For either redesign action, a study of the future, in relation to the present, will be needed before final redesign action can be taken.

As a final step, new plans are written as in the earlier "utilization" stage. Activities during the revitalization stage, therefore, prepare for the needs of the future and set the course once again. This charting of a new course is accomplished by initiating the original stages of the planning process (exploration, distillation and utilization) and incorporating them into revitalization activities.

Toward a New Planning Future

While these six planning elements—dedication, exploration, distillation, utilization, characterization, and revitalization—do require concentration of time and attention they, nevertheless, effect the best operational administration presently known and one that is seen as a hope for education's future (Mauriel, 1989). For planning of an integrative curriculum, the utilization of such an approach is far superior to "pre-packaged" direction currently given to school staffs concerning new practices. It has been the contention of this paper that, in response to the pressing curricular need, administrators will need to adopt the *planning* approach, described above, rather than the *prescribed* approach, as currently practiced. The *planning* approach assumes proactive attention to the future issues of program, staffing, funding, materials and facilities, whereas the *prescribed* approach, however expedient, results in cursory, piecemeal, and reactive approaches to serious problems.

Addressing Perceived Constraints and Possible Roadblocks
to Planning

As has been stated earlier in this paper, a shortage of resources needed to carry out the planning frequently prevents educational administrators from attempting comprehensive planning. Part of the problem is that the exact amount and kind of resources needed for long-range planning are unknown.

Shortage of Resources

By describing resources needed for planning, fears about unrealistic requirements can be allayed. For the most part, resource needs for comprehensive planning, at district or site levels are, primarily, the use of staff time. At the site level, some solutions for the need of staff involvement in the planning process can include: (1) staff time obtained by utilization of regular staff meetings; (2) staff utilized by contractual arrangement, for three one-day working sessions at 3-week intervals; or (3) staff utilized in planning sessions during minimum days. What generally prevents the utilization of these resources is that there has been a general failure in recognizing the value of "buying" planning time. A lack of acknowledgement for needed planning time relates not only to comprehensive planning processes but planning in all areas of education, including time for teachers to plan their instructional programs.

Therefore, the foremost problem with resource availability is recognition and acceptance of the need—*not* a lack of resources. Once needs are recognized, a re-prioritization of resource allocation and disbursement can serve the needs. Of course, requisite to a comprehensive planning action is the need for superordinates and subordinates, as well as other actors—such as union representatives and community groups—to be informed concerning the critical role of planning, "dedicated" to the planning agenda, and enthusiastic about the long-term savings to be gained from appropriate planning. This information will precipitate a "dedication," as described earlier in the paper, to the planning agenda and will result in enthusiasm about long-term savings obtained from appropriate planning.

Time Management

Once the importance for a focus of resources has been acknowledged, time management, for most administrators, becomes a much-diminished issue. Once the decision to plan has been made, the process of arranging time slots for the planning is much more manageable. Therefore, "dedication" becomes the all-important element which addresses both the problems of time management and resource allocation. Once the needs for planning are known and accepted, the contribution and rearrangement of time becomes much less a factor. The importance, then, in reaching for the level of comprehensive planning is to review and re-order priorities.

Summary

The accomplishment of an integrative curriculum has been described as necessitating large-scale, careful and long-term planning processes. Because this planning will involve total school staffs, it has been determined that it becomes an administrative responsibility to gain knowledge of the requirements for an integrative curriculum and of planning processes which can assist staff in designing and implementing the curriculum. Progressive administrators, no doubt, want to become knowledgeable in planning or "planning literate." In attempting planning literacy, there are a few obstacles which face all administrators. Major among the problems are how to find the time and the resources and how to involve those primary resources—staff and community—in the planning process. All of these obstacles can be overcome by the initial force of dedication, accompanied by the desire to do something for educational systems and educational constituencies which is superior to current educational practice and current educational learning situations.

References

Blair, B. G. (1990). *Teacher survey.* San Bernardino, CA: California State University.

Dressel, P. (1958). The meaning and significance of integration. In N. Henry (Ed.), *The integration of educational experiences, the fifty-seventh yearbook of the National Society for the Study of Education.* Chicago: The University of Chicago Press.

Drucker, P. F. (1974). *Management: Tasks, responsibilities, practices.* New York: Harper and Row.

Harter, P. D., & Gehrke, N. J. (1989). Integrative curriculum: A kaleidoscope of alternatives. *Educational Horizons, 68*(1), 12-17.

Holmberg, S. F. (1979). *Failing to plan is planning to fail.* Washington, DC: American University, School of Business Administration.

Mauriel, J. J. (1989). *Strategic leadership for schools.* San Francisco: Jossey-Bass.

Turner, F. (1986, September). Design for a new academy. *Harper's,* pp. 49-52.

Whitehead, A. (1929). *The aims of education and other essays.* New York: Macmillan.

How do children make choices which then guide their own thoughts and ability to create new meanings? The literature suggests that children form cognitive frameworks which help them organize and integrate new and unfamiliar information. The author explores the formation of concepts in children and the power of these concepts to further learning. In particular, the paper looks at children's conceptual frameworks as they move through varying stages of complexity. A preliminary research report invites students to create cognitive maps which include emotional as well as attitudinal aspects of their own views and formed concepts. As we begin to more deeply understand children's thoughts, their emotional world, and the constructs which have meaning for them, we can begin to connect more meaningfully with the world that exists for them and can learn better to gently and intelligently guide them from where they are.

TEACHING FOR CONCEPTUAL CHANGE

Phyllis Maxey Fernlund

When individuals learn, they integrate their experience into their own unique understanding of the world. Sources of the experience may be everyday life, a book, or the state-authorized school curriculum, but meaning is created by the learner. In this paper I would like to explore implications of recent work in conceptual change for teachers, and teachers of social studies in particular.

In the study of the individual learner, constructivists have emphasized the active role of the learner in creating meaning. As the brain seeks patterns among objects and events, these patterns are captured in concepts. This "meaning-making" can be seen as embedded in a cognitive structure or framework which acts as a filter to ignore or incorporate new information. "The continuous flow of experience is punctuated . . . by the conceptual organization of such experiences" (Pines, 1985, p. 108). Concepts can be seen as human inventions that reflect a person's unique combination of personal knowledge with formal knowledge. Concepts are part of larger frameworks that can change as a result of new information, new analogies, or the resolution of incompatible ideas.

The "Vines" Metaphor

Vygotsky (1962) identifies two sources of knowledge in the individual. One is knowledge acquired in interacting with the environment. It is a person's own "sense making of the environment she observes, tempered and manipulated by her interaction with parents, peers, television, and other influences (West & Pines, 1985). The other source of knowledge is disciplined knowledge, external to the individual, generated by people considered to be authorities in their field. This is often the knowledge base for school curriculum and textbooks. Vygotsky envisions the upward development of a child's spontaneous concepts as experiences and language develop. Scientific concepts, taught by explicit instruction, proceed downward, abstractions moving to a more concrete level, from definitions to examples.

West and Pines use a metaphor of two vines to understand the interaction of personal knowledge and formal knowledge.

> We imagine two vines representing these different sources of knowledge, the one originating from the learner's intuitive knowledge of the world (which we call the upward-growing vine to emphasize that this is part of the growth of the learner), and the other originating from formal instruction (which we call the downward-growing vine to emphasize its imposition on the learner from above). Genuine conceptual learning involves the intertwining of these two vines. (West & Pines, 1985, p. 3)

A teacher's plan of instruction must take into account three possible situations for students who are to learn new information.

1. *Conflict situation:* Both vines are well-developed, but the child's personal cognitive framework is in conflict with the curricular content.

2. *Congruent situation:* Both vines are well-established, and the child can easily assimilate the school knowledge with personal knowledge.

3. *Symbolic knowledge situation:* Upward vine of personal knowledge has a few runners to interact with the downward (school knowledge) vine.

The vine metaphor is a useful way to portray the interaction between the experiences the learner brings to the classroom and the teacher's translation of the formal knowledge of the curriculum. It also captures the image of growth. The acquisition of concepts is never complete. It is an ongoing process throughout a person's life.

The individual determines what happens to the new knowledge that comes from experience or from formal instruction. The new information can be ignored because there is no part of the vine that enables it to get a foothold. Or it can be dismissed because of dissonance created with existing patterns. The new knowledge can be memorized by students but it is not integrated into their conceptual frameworks. If the teacher gives the test quickly enough, test results may give the appearance that learning has taken place when, in fact, there has been no integration of the old and new, and the new is quickly forgotten. The formal instruction is not used by students to make sense of the world.

The "Mosaic" Metaphor

Head and Sutton (1985) use the metaphor of a "mosaic" to explore the individual nature of cognitive structures and the barriers to change. The tiles in a person's mosaic are limited by language and experience. The accumulated cognitions build the mosaic and help define the individuality of the person. As a conceptual framework is linked with personal identity, we might expect change in a child's cognitive framework to occur if his or her identity is strengthened. Making sense of one's experience is emotionally satisfying. Head and Sutton argue that as the mosaic forms, there is an emotional commitment to that way of understanding the world. When curricular content creates conflict between the personal mosaic and school knowledge, a student may resist a more scholarly perspective coming from the disciplines.

The patterns built into an individual's cognitive mosaic serve to reduce the confusion and vast complexity of life. Head and Sutton illustrate this process:

For example, once you have come to the view that the state of the nation is accounted for by the existence of "Reds under the beds" all further information will be processed accordingly. Already at this point, we begin to see how commitment grows out of particular cognitions, and in turn will shape further development of the cognitive structures. (p. 92)

In making sense of experience, the individual may be overwhelmed by its complexity. One way to handle that complexity is to operate within a framework, inside a theory that screens information in a particular way. The mosaic metaphor portrays the ridigity that may be a part of a student's cognitive framework.

Conceptual Change and Stages

Individual conceptual frameworks are also affected by age-related progressions in understanding, changes which the teacher and school curriculum will not be able to drastically alter. In a study of children in southern England, Furth (1980) found that there were definite age-related conceptual shifts in understanding the social world. Personalistic elaborations of government were typical of 5-6 year olds, a finding echoed in other research on political socialization. For these young children, government authority was housed in one person, the Council representative, the mayor, God or Jesus. As one seven year old explained:

> *Child:* "Council, the man, he tells the people where the houses should be."
> *Interviewer:* "How does he know?"
> *Child:* "Because he is a precious man and God and Jesus and the mayor—they know where things are." (p. 43)

For 9-10 year olds, Furth found a view of government that allows for different functions, but these are not integrated into an internal framework.

> *Child:* "Council pays doctors, for all kinds of things, nurses, firemen."
> *Interviewer:* "Where do they get the money?"
> *Child:* "I never knew that, I am interested in finding that out." (p. 44)

By the age of 10 or 11, Furth found that children viewed government as a provider of services for which people paid taxes. A thirteen year old explained: "Police get paid by the government and he pays income tax back to them out of a small amount of his wages, so that the government can still carry on going and get money from other people to pay him" (p. 46). Government authority is undifferentiated for some children from religious authority. Government is the supreme law, the job-giver and distributor. As children grow older, they differentiate social functions and develop frameworks that describe still incomplete social systems. Furth argues that a systematic framework of "political and community understanding is hardly present below age 12 and develops slowly during adolescence" (p. 86).

Furth's observations follow the expansion in conceptual understanding described by Vygotsky (1962) in three stages: (1) the child merges diverse elements into one unarticulated image, (2) the child's thinking is in complexes, objects are united in a child's mind by subjective impressions and direct experience, and (3) the child uses abstract logical thought, conceptual structure is based on single principles.

Although Furth argues for a stage-like shift in understanding, Keil's (1989) research indicates that children's thinking varies with the kind of concept. He did not find an across-the-board shift for all concepts; change occurred two or more years earlier for some concepts than for others.

Keil (1989) has investigated the shift that occurs when children are able to identify the defining features of a concept and weigh those more heavily than the characteristic features. Defining features are properties that are necessary and sufficient for describing an instance of a concept. Characteristic features are not necessary, but are highly characteristic. For example, in one of his studies the concept of "island" was described with the correct defining feature, but uncharacteristic features as well:

(Correct example) On this piece of land, there are apartment buildings, snow, and no green things growing. This piece of land is surrounded by water on all sides. Could that be an island?

(Nonexample of concept: There is this place that sticks out of the land like a finger. Coconut trees and palm trees grow there and the girls sometimes wear flowers in their hair because it's so warm all the time. There is water on all sides except one. Could that be an island? (Keil, p. 71)

The shift to defining features came earlier with moral concepts such as cheating, lying and stealing. The majority of Kindergartners could identify the defining features of such concepts and were not confused by characteristic features. Concepts that were concerned with kinship and cooking did not show the characteristic to defining shift until children were in grades 2-4. It is interesting to note that when mothers of these children gave specific instruction that emphasized the defining features, the children treated this information as another characteristic. There was a definite developmental pattern in their understanding, but not a global shift for all concepts at the same time. The research on the individual disciplines, "school" knowledge, is just beginning to identify age-related shifts, as well as the resistance to conceptual change (Anderson, 1989; Gilbert, Watts, Osborne, 1985).

Applications to Teaching

The teacher takes expert knowledge from the curriculum and, in interactions with students, helps children make that knowledge their own so that it is useful in understanding their world. Research in cognitive psychology often looks at the individual learner, a focus that is a luxury for the classroom teacher. The teacher is faced with groups of children, with a social context for learning. Herndon (1971) gives us a vivid picture of a teacher's job as sorting out the winners and losers in a never-ending game:

You deal with children in groups. You teach first graders to read. You write *ch* on the board, and ask [sic] who knows how this sounds? Some kids already know and raise their hands with tremendous relief. They are going to make it this year. Others think they know but they aren't sure (Maybe *ch* has changed since their mamas told them). Others never heard of it. They might be happy to know what it sounds like (why not?) but at the same time they see that a lot of other smart kids already know.

Then for awhile in the primary grades the school will try to teach those who didn't know it already. But it doesn't work. It doesn't work because the winners keep intruding, raising their hands in advance of the question, or because while the teacher works with the losers on what the winners already know the winners are free to read and draw and talk to one another and therefore learn other stuff. . . . Later on, of course, the school will refuse to teach the losers at all. (p. 83)

Let's imagine two different jobs for the teacher. In the first assignment the teacher imposes someone else's curriculum demands on children, and then tests to see who has memorized the "content" and who has not. S/he then assigns grades of D and F to students who may face the following barriers: (1) they have no schema for understanding the formal knowledge in the school curriculum (there is no upward-growing vine); (2) they have a conceptual framework that could be activated, but the teacher did not tap into this framework; (3) they are not yet able to handle the intellectual tasks demanded, but will be able to succeed in another year or two, (4) they feel too threatened to learn, (5) they did, in fact, expand their conceptual understanding, but the teacher's test did not measure it.

The second teacher's job is quite different from what Herndon describes. S/he is required to implement curriculum guidelines, but not to label a child a success or failure through grades, grouping arrangements, or rewards for those who already know the content. S/he must teach a unit on the Middle Ages in a way that allows every seventh grader to have a richer understanding of that period of time.

S/he uses literature and video to tell tales about the problems a medieval household faced in dealing with bugs, rancid meat, garbage, and a host of other situations that children can understand. The class builds a castle in their classroom including stained glass windows and a paper dungeon. Fiction and nonfiction books are available. Dramatic scenes in which the king must sign a Magna Carta, sharing power with his nobles are re-enacted. After watching an instructional television program, "Newscasts from the Past," the students create their own news show from June 15, 1215, and report on events from around the world at that moment in time. On the day of the videotaping, each student comes in a simple costume of those times. Students have chosen a special area to research and they serve as resources for information about medieval clothing, weapons, criminal trials, housekeeping, religious practices, and royalty. The computer is used to print a timeline that contains some of the products of their research. The unit takes eight weeks.

The second teacher has planned a course of study that can tap many different schemata of her children—beginning with simple human acts such as ways of cooking and fighting during the Middle Ages in Europe, and moving to historically important moments such as the signing of the Magna Carta. S/he has changed the emphasis on winners and losers to a learning situation that uses the talents, knowledge, and interests of all of the students. Their cooperative projects in making the video newscast and in transforming their classroom into a castle bring the history of long ago into their imaginations, and provide concrete examples of the abstractions in the history textbook.

Assessing Conceptual Frameworks

How does the teacher measure student achievement, so that children and parents have a picture of their efforts? (Future employers and institutions of higher education can do their own testing). Much paper and pencil testing seems to conceal how little students really know. Many testing procedures do not tell us very much about how students are thinking or what they know. In developing alternatives to multiple choice biology tests, Anderson (1989) found that "actual student responses, especially longer written responses that reveal students' reasoning, tend to confront the reader with the qualitative reality of students' thinking" (p. 70). There is a great need for instruments that help us understand conceptual change and growth. I will suggest three possible tools for the teacher.

Concept maps. Concept maps help indicate the complexity of a child's understanding. Maps, webs, or clusters are all terms for a graphic representation of the relationships between concepts. Concept maps are often used in language arts as a pre-writing activity, and many children are now familiar with this strategy. Novak and Gowin (1984) have used concept maps for curriculum planning, student study tools, evaluation, and research.

The teacher can use concept maps for preassessment and postassessment. S/he might begin by drawing a circle on the board and asking students to draw connecting circles, adding as many links as they can to this word. At the beginning of the history unit, the teacher could place the word medieval or Middle Ages in the center circle, and let children add whatever they can think of that relates to that concept, sharing their ideas with each other. These concept maps could be saved until the end of the unit. Children's maps are often far more complex and involved by the end of the unit, and show new associations that have been activated by their study. At the end of the unit, the two maps could be compared to show students the growth in their understanding.

I.A.I. A strategy to measure the interaction between children's personal knowledge and formal knowledge as been used by Gilbert, Watts, and Osborne (1985) in their work with science students. The Interview-about-Instances (I.A.I.) consists of a tape-recorded discussion between the researcher and student, using a deck of cards that explore certain concepts. In their investigation of science students' understanding of "force," one of the cards pictured a person riding a bike followed by three statements: no pedalling, no brakes, and the bike is slowing down. The question on the card was, "Is there force on the bike?" The concern here is with the student's own interpretation, the "student's science" which combines children's common sense understanding with the teacher's instruction based on "scientists' science." In analyzing the results, the researchers paid particular attention to two kinds of student talk: "First, it includes talk that expands the conceptual framework of ideas; and second, it includes all the talk that alludes to projections, speculations, or consequences of the situation depicted on the cards" (p. 22). These researchers found that some children retained their intuitive ideas regardless of the formal instruction. Others were in transition between nonscientific conceptions and those acceptable to scientists. In using the I.A.I., they were seeking students' integration of knowledge, the ways students made sense of a scientific concept.

Student talk. If a teacher believes that children construct their own knowledge and then use that framework to make sense of the world, the language of students will be of significance. It can show the presence or absence or progression of conceptual change that incorporates the curricular content. Throughout a semester or year, changes in the interaction between personal and formal knowledge may be seen in the way students talk about concepts, problems and events.

Of course, teachers do not have the luxury of talking at length with all students one-on-one, transcribing the dialogue, and poring over the transcripts as does a researcher. But the teacher could look at student talk as more than just the presence or absence of the right answer. Important concepts will be taught and used again and again. It would be an interesting assessment of learning if the teacher would track a student's progress in using scientific language and explanations over time. An open-ended question—short answer or essay—on the same concept could be a part of a written examination at the end of several units. Student discourse at three or four points in time in the course could be examined for its complexity and incorporation of scientists' science.

Let's apply this to our seventh grade history teacher, and the study of the Middle Ages in Europe. As a curriculum goal, s/he might want students to understand the concepts of technology and technological change. Using a picture of the building of a castle or cathedral, the teacher might ask an exam question such as, "Is anyone in this picture using technology? In what ways? What does technology mean? Another question may address the subject of technological change, asking for students' theories on why such changes occurred at that time. When studying later units on the Renaissance and European exploration, similar questions might be asked and compared with student dialogue earlier in the year.

If the teacher views learning as individual problem solving—a search for a theory that makes sense, explains events, feelings, experiences—then it is vital to find out what theories students currently have. Perhaps the teacher wants to explore social science explanations of how technology affects social institutions throughout her history course. Preassessment of students' theories might include a writing prompt such as, "How would your life be different if the only form of transportation was the bicycle? No cars, no trucks, no school buses, no trains, no planes, no space shuttles." The teacher can use preassessment information such as the writing prompt to discover "students' science" and plan how he will introduce "scientists' science," the scholarly and scientific explanations of the impact of technology on societies. The teacher's plan must be informed by the upward-growing vines, the personal knowledge base of the students.

Conceptual Frameworks: Research in Progress

This author is currently engaged in an exploratory study of the political understanding of eighth grade students as they encounter a state-required history unit on the U.S. Constitution. Students from eight classrooms in three middle schools located in the greater Los Angeles area participated in the study. Students drew concept maps on "democracy" before and after the unit. Concept maps on the "constitution" were drawn after their study was completed. A structured sample of 60 students was selected to include diverse ethnic groups and gender balance. This smaller sample, drawn from the eight classrooms, participated in individual interviews ranging from thirty to forty-five minutes.

Figures 1 through 3 portray several concept maps drawn by these eighth grade students. The diversity of conceptual frameworks as indicated in these concept maps brings to mind the vines metaphor. In Figure 1 the students, who have not yet formally studied the Constitution, have many different concept maps on "democracy." In some cases, the students' upward growing vines seem to have few runners to absorb the new knowledge on constitutional government that they will study. In four cases, students were unable to make any associations with the word democracy in the center. Others have a fairly elaborate schema for the concepts with eight or more associations. The most frequently chosen links with the word democracy were: voting, government, First Amendment freedoms, freedom, the Presidency, and law.

For the eighth graders in Figure 2 who had already studied the Constitution, the concept of democracy was frequently linked to ideas of freedom, voting, choices, constitution, justice and fairness. Students created maps with as many as 21 links. There are more maps in this group that show a hierarchy of concepts, subconcepts and examples. Their maps show a complex structure of relationships, in contrast to maps in which students draw a simple wheel with unrelated concepts arranged as spokes around the wheel.

In Figure 3, the word "Constitution" was the focus of the concept map for these students who had just completed a four-week unit on the Constitution. Students frequently mentioned the Bill of Rights, amendments, branches of government and laws, but did not include their attitudes and feelings in response to the "Constitution" stimulus. There are rather elaborate categories and hierarchies of concepts and subconcepts in some cases. The maps contained as many as twenty-five associations.

Cognitive maps include the emotional and attitudinal aspects of creating meaning. You can see in some of the maps negative and positive associations with law and government. If the maps are used before the study of the Constitution, the teacher can see what knowledge, attitudes and beliefs students are bringing to the study. One measure of conceptual change that will be investigated at the completion of their formal study of the Constitution is a comparison of the maps before and after the unit is completed. Maps can be evaluated using various criteria: the number of links, the structure used by the student, the accuracy and comprehensiveness of the maps.

The Island Questionnaire

In addition to the concept maps, a sample of students are responding to a questionnaire (Gallatin, 1985) that taps into student thinking about government and law. The interview questions are based on this scenario:

> I want you to imagine that about a thousand people became dissatisfied with the way things were going in their country. They decided to leave their country. They got together and purchased an island in the Pacific and moved there. As soon as they arrived, they realized they would have to set up some sort of government—to make laws, rules and regulations. The questions I'm going to ask you will be about the problems they ran into. Do you understand? Do you have any questions you want to ask before I go on?

The reason for using a hypothetical like this is to avoid asking direct knowledge-based recall questions which might force a student to often respond, "I Don't Know." It also provides opportunities to see the student's reasoning when presented with problem situations.

It is too early to report complete findings, but the interviews to date provide a picture of the naivete, humor, and wisdom of some of the eighth graders before they have formally studied the Constitution. The last question of the interview asks them to describe their ideal society and government. In the interview they have just finished thinking about the island's government in which executive, legislative, and judicial functions are housed in one body, a Council of 20 elected people.

In discussing their vision of the ideal government, students recommended:

A boy: I would have a Council of about 20-30 people who would change every week so like everybody would get a chance, then if they didn't like [the laws they passed], they could wait for their chance.

A boy: I'd be the leader for 10 years and then retire. I would want a Council in my government so that if one person forgets something, others can remind him.

A girl: I don't know. I would want a government where I could ask for their help and they could help me.

A boy: I want a president with a limit of two terms in office. The Council needs to have a yearly write-in thing so that people that disagree, write it on paper, and it will go straight to the Council. They will look at it and try to fix it.

A girl: I want people from all classes on the Council, not just rich people. I would have 25 people on the Council and they would also be the judges because they know what to do and will be able to settle it without favoritism or anything.

It will be interesting to see if the study of the Constitution produces any changes in their present understanding and misunderstanding of how democratic government works. As they study the political concerns and solutions of James Madison and other framers of the Constitution, will these eighth graders be able to integrate this formal knowledge into their own thinking?

Conclusion

If education is to move beyond the memorization of "school knowledge," we need to pay increased attention to what children know as they begin to learn a subject. The intuitive understanding of children must be integrated with the theories and concepts of the disciplines, if formal instruction is to benefit children. A teacher who works with large groups in the classroom needs a rich supply of resources beyond the textbook to expand children's understanding. A teacher needs time to listen to children, to reflect on their language and their thinking. Assessment needs to reflect the processes of assimilation, accommodation and conceptual change, so that great effort is not expended to teach content that will be forgotten within days. The child's conceptual framework, the child's personal knowledge has been greatly overshadowed by the adult frameworks of textbook writers and experts in the disciplines and in curriculum. The teacher is the creative, vitally important mediator who adjusts the curriculum to children's reality.

As teachers we want to know if our instruction is producing meaningful learning or superficial knowledge that will be easily forgotten. How do students make sense of the information presented in class, in textbooks, on television? How can we find out what students within the same grade as well as students of different ages bring to the study of a subject? Are these concepts that students are not ready to learn at a particular age? Are there new ways to teach and measure the kind of learning that creates conceptual change? Instruments drawn from research in cognitive psychology provide opportunities for a renewed focus on the role of the student in the learning process. It is my hope that this new direction in research can give teachers new tools to make the formal knowledge of the curriculum meaningful to students.

References

Anderson, C. W. (1989). Assessing student understanding of biological concepts. In W. G. Rosen (Ed.), *High school biology today and tomorrow* (pp. 55-72). Washington, DC: National Academy Press.

Furth, H. G. (1980). *The world of grown-ups: Children's conceptions of society.* New York: Elsevier.

Gallatin, J. (1985). *Democracy's children: The development of political thinking in adolescents.* Ann Arbor, MI: Quod Publishing Co.

Gilbert, J. K., Watts, D. M., Osborne, R. J. (1985). Eliciting student views using an interview-about-instances technique. In L. West & A. Pines (Eds.), *Cognitive structure and conceptual change* (pp. 11-28). Orlando: Academic Press.

Head, J. O., & Sutton, C. R. (1985). Language, understanding, and commitment. In L. West & A. Pines (Eds.), *Cognitive structure and conceptual change* (pp. 91-100). Orlando: Academic Press.

Herndon, J. (1971). *How to survive in your native land.* New York: Simon & Schuster.

Keil, F. C. (1989). *Concepts, kinds and cognitive development.* Cambridge, MA: M.I.T. Press.

Novak, J. D., & Gowin, D. B. (1984). *Learning how to learn.* Cambridge: Cambridge University Press.

Pines, A. L. (1985). Toward a taxonomy of conceptual relations and the implications for the evaluation of cognitive structures. In L. West & A. Pines (Eds.), *Cognitive structure and conceptual change* (pp. 101-116). Orlando: Academic Press.

Vygotsky, L. S. (1962). *Thought and language.* Cambridge, MA: M.I.T. Press.

West, L. H. T., & Pines, A. L. (Eds.). (1985). *Cognitive structure and conceptual change.* Orlando: Academic Press.

Within the construct of integrative learning, classroom management requires reconceptualization. The following paper proposes a model for classroom management which integrates theories from two separate disciplines, clinical psychology and business management. The model accounts for teacher belief systems which influence the use of power and control, as well as attitudes toward responsibility for tasks and relationships.

A unique feature of the model is that it links student maturity with task expectations and defines different approaches to management on the basis of the match between student maturity level and task demands.

RECONCEPTUALIZING
CLASSROOM MANAGEMENT
Barbara Larrivee

Introduction

Classroom management is a multidimensional construct. Several conditions are integral to effective classroom management. They include: (1) Creating a stimulating and supportive setting for learning to occur, (2) establishing reasonable expectations based on consideration of student characteristics, and (3) providing opportunities for all students to experience success.

Effective classroom management is inextricably tied to the quality of educational experiences in which students engage as well as the teacher's skill in organizing the class structure to facilitate efficient teaching and learning. In order to be effective, the classroom teacher needs to conceptualize classroom management from a perspective that is comprehensive, holistic, and developmental, incorporating both managerial tasks as well as concern for student personal growth and development. This broadened concept of classroom management calls for a transformation of the role of the teacher from "controller" to "facilitator." The role of the teacher becomes one of providing a learning environment which supports student problem solving efforts by helping students expand their cognitive awareness and behavioral response repertoire by offering students nonevaluative interpretations of their behavior and developing problem solving strategies, adaptive skills, and student autonomy.

While many authors have recognized that classroom management is a broader issue than controlling student behavior (e.g., Charles, 1989; Gordon, 1974; Grossman, 1990; Kounin, 1970; Larrivee, 1992), traditionally classroom management has focused on the organizational or structural aspects of management. Thus, effective classroom management is seen as tantamount to controlling student behavior, calling for appropriate teacher intervention to modify student behavior. Furthermore, student behavior is often determined to be appropriate or inappropriate in isolation from consideration of the learning task at hand and/or performance expectations.

Models of classroom management currently in vogue emanate from the body of research known as the teacher effectiveness literature. This database supports the position that increased achievement is related to high teacher control of time allocations and a high degree of attention to task (e.g., Brophy, 1979; Brophy & Evertson, 1974; Brophy & Good, 1986; Gage, 1978; Gersten, Woodward, & Darch, 1986; Medley, 1977; Rosenshine, 1979; Rosenshine & Berliner, 1978; Rosenshine & Stevens, 1984; Slavin, Karweit, & Madden, 1989). The "direct instruction" model as conceptualized by Rosenshine (1979) is an attempt to capture the results of this research literature and is actually a model of teacher control (Crocker & Brooker, 1986). Classroom management viewed within this framework focuses primarily on the structure and control dimensions of effective management.

The model being proposed here is an attempt to broaden the concept of classroom management beyond organizational tasks and behavior control to include consideration for student personal growth and development as well as pose an interactive model which incorporates individual student characteristics, curriculum appropriateness, and performance expectations.

Conceptual Framework

This paper proposes a model for reconceptualizing classroom management based on the integration of theories from two different disciplines, namely clinical psychology and business management. The model merges an attribution theory model for helping and coping with situational leadership theory. In the model, four styles of helping are defined based on attributions of blame and control. These four styles are then aligned with the intersecting constructs of task directiveness, socio-emotional support, and follower maturity from situational leadership theory to construct a model which bridges these two theories into a new paradigm for considering classroom management. The model offers a multidimensional perspective for understanding management principles and considering teacher belief systems.

Attribution Theory Model for Helping and Coping

Brickman, Rabinowitz, Karuza, Coates, Cohn, and Kidder (1982) have posited that interaction styles for helping and coping are defined by attributions of blame and control. A person either blames or holds another person responsible for his/her predicament or believes that the person's problem is due to circumstances beyond their control; that is, s/he either attributes blame or does not attribute blame. In their model, there is a parallel dichotomous relationship relative to responsibility for solving problems. A person views others as either willing and/or capable of providing a reasonable solution to their problem or not willing and/or incapable of providing a solution; that is, s/he either attributes control or fails to attribute control to the person experiencing the problem. The intersecting attributions of blame and control produce four general orientations to helping.

Brickman et al. defined these different styles as: the medical style in which the person is held responsible for neither the problem nor the solution; the moral style in which the person is responsible for both the problem and the solution; the compensatory style where the person is not blamed for his/her predicament but is expected to find a reasonable solution; and the enlightenment style where the person is held accountable for their problem but is considered incapable of producing an appropriate solution. The model being proposed here represents a redefining of the four helping styles of Brickman et al. to provide greater congruence with educational terminology while preserving the construct of attributions of blame and control.

Applying the model to classroom management, teacher helping styles would be based on the interaction of perceived blame, that is the teacher's attribution of responsibility to students for the learning and behavior problems they exhibit, and perceived control or attribution of responsibility to students for finding solutions to their problems. The intersection of these attributions of blame and control define four approaches to helping in the classroom setting. As shown in Figure 1, the first quadrant, the power model, depicts a style predicated on power and authority. Teacher vigilance is required at all times; students are viewed as responsible for their problems and as unable or unwilling to exercise control and/or find solutions to their problems. In the treatment model, the problem is attributed to forces outside the student's control (e.g., psychological, environmental, biological) and thus requires expert treatment. The assumption is that the student is responsible for neither the problem nor the solution. These two styles are teacher-directed and serve to solve problems for students.

In quadrant three, the moral style, the student is held personally responsible for his or her predicament, as either a result of complacency or choice. Additionally, the student is expected to find a reasonable solution to the situation or problem. The teacher remains relatively detached, providing little guidance, but encourages students to succeed by virtue of their own initiative and hard work. The philosophy which drives this style is that "the world is just a place where you get what you deserve." In the facilitative quadrant, while the student is viewed as not responsible for his or her problem, the student is perceived as capable of ultimately finding a solution to his or her predicament. The teacher's role is to facilitate, locate and allocate resources to students, provide ongoing support, foster student autonomy, and assist students in developing necessary skills. Both the moral and facilitative styles are viewed as student-centered in that they ultimately give responsibility to students for solving their own problems. Figure 2 defines the role of both the teacher and the student for each of the management styles.

Teacher beliefs about their primary role with respect to classroom management will clearly influence their behavior control styles. Students' needs relative to classroom control are conceived in quite different veins dependent on the model one espouses. In the power model, teachers believe students need discipline, whereas in the treatment model, teachers think students need help. Likewise, in the moral model, students need only to be motivated and in the facilitative model students need to be empowered. The allocation of classroom management techniques to each style represents an extension of the alignment offered by Chrystal (1988). Figure 3 provides a mapping of classroom behavior management approaches which fall within each of the four styles.

In the model, the concept of control is equated with the teacher's perception of the student's ability to provide *right* or *good* solutions. If the teacher believes the student will not provide an appropriate solution, then s/he imposes a solution (power model). If, on the other hand, the teacher believes the student is not capable of providing a solution, then the teacher provides adaptations, either in task structure or performance expectation (treatment model). In both cases, the teacher exercises control or applies structure. The blame component defines the teacher's perception of responsibility for the learning and/or behavior problems which students exhibit. If the teacher holds students responsible, again s/he either provides control or gives the solution (power model) or lets students choose (moral model). Given a choice, students either make an appropriate choice, or an inappropriate choice, in which case the teacher still supports the student (as an individual while rejecting the behavior) but may apply a mutually agreed-upon consequence. Conversely, when teachers think students are not responsible for their predicament, they can either take responsibility for a solution (treatment model) or support the student's autonomy (facilitative model). When students are lacking the necessary repertoire of behavioral responses to make an appropriate choice, then the teacher may need to teach the students the skill(s) they are lacking; that is, engage in skill building so that the students will eventually become more capable of making better choices in the future.

Situational Leadership Theory

The second component of this model aligns the four styles based on attributions of blame and control with the intersecting constructs of task directiveness, socio-emotional support, and follower maturity from situational leadership theory. Effective leadership style theory advances the premise that there is no single, all-purpose leadership style that is most effective; successful leaders are those who can adapt their behavior to meet the demands of their own unique environment. Leadership style is the consistent pattern of behavior exhibited when attempting to influence the activities of others. The pattern generally involves either task behavior or relationship behavior, or some combination of both. These two types of behavior are central to the concept of leadership style. Task behavior is the extent to which a leader organizes and defines the roles of individuals and members of his/her group by explaining what activities each is to do as well as when, where and how tasks are to be accomplished. Relationship behavior is the extent to which a leader engages in personal relationships with individuals or members of his or her group, that is, the amount of socio-emotional support provided by the leader as well as the extent to which the leader engages in interpersonal communications and facilitating behaviors. In education, a parallel distinction has been made between teacher-directed management behavior and student-centered management behavior.

Situational leadership theory is based on a relationship between the amount of direction (task behavior) and the amount of socio-emotional support (relationship behavior) a leader provides, and the followers' level of maturity (Hersey & Blanchard, 1972). Maturity is defined as the capacity to set high but attainable goals, willingness and ability to take responsibility, and education and/or experience of an individual or group. Situational leadership theory holds that these aspects of maturity should be considered *only* in relation to a specific task to be performed. That is, an individual or a group is not mature or immature in any global sense, but only in terms of a specific task. According to situational leadership theory, as the level of maturity of followers continues to increase in terms of accomplishing a specific task, leaders should begin to reduce their task behavior and increase their relationship behavior until the group is sufficiently mature for the leaders to decrease their relationship behavior as well. The theory basically purports that as followers become more capable of accomplishing the task without direction from the leader, task direction can be minimized while personal support is strengthened (see Figure 4). Thus, this theory aligns the appropriateness or effectiveness of a leadership style with the task-relevant maturity of the followers. Applying situational leadership theory to classroom control would translate to students requiring greater amounts of directiveness or teacher control when they are not able to perform a task independently or without teacher guidance.

Traditionally in education, teacher-directed and student-centered styles have been considered in dichotomous terms, rather than aligning styles with student variables (such as task demands). There has been a long history of operating on the assumption that there is an inverse relationship between teacher warmth (i.e., positive affect, emotional climate, learner support) and teacher

control (i.e., directiveness, structure, organization) (Larrivee, 1985). Teacher
warmth is generally defined operationally in terms of the tendency of the teacher
to be approving, provide emotional support, encourage, reassure and commend,
express considerable understanding, and accept the feelings of students. The
directive dimension typically defines the teacher as a dominant, controlling
figure, providing overall organization, issuing directives, lecturing, providing
factual information, and asking factual recall questions.

A review of instruments used over the years to assess these dimensions
reveals a pattern of eliding the two dimensions—that is, directiveness and
warmth on the part of the teacher have been collapsed into a single dimension
representing the teacher on a continuum from "teacher-centered" to "learner-
centered." This conceptual confusion is apparent beginning with the work of
Lewin, Lippitt, and White (1939) in early studies of group dynamics in which
an "autocratic-democratic" dichotomy was utilized. At about the same time,
Anderson (1939) began applying similar concepts to the study of teaching
behaviors. His research was designed to study the effects of "dominative" versus
"integrative" teacher behaviors. Withall's (1949) instrument for measuring the
social-emotional climate of classrooms is based on a ratio of "learner-centered"
to "teacher-centered" behaviors. And Flanders (1967) defined teacher influence
as "direct" or "indirect."

An implied assumption underlying this dichotomous view is that warmth
and directiveness are negatively correlated. For example, in Flanders Interaction
Analysis Categories system (FIAC), direct influence consists of "stating the
teacher's own opinion or ideas, directing the pupil's action, criticizing his
behavior, or justifying the teacher's authority or use of that authority." Thus,
providing direction for the student and criticizing the student both contribute to
a single factor.

Although Dunkin and Biddle (1974) documented support for the
independence of the two concepts of warmth and directiveness when they

reported that three out of four independent studies they reviewed found teacher "indirectness" to be unrelated to "directness," the conceptual confusion persisted. Again, Soar and Soar (1979) referenced this issue, advocating the independence of the two factors. While the two constructs of warmth and control are different, they are potentially compatible. The application of this line of thinking to this model is that a teacher may need to provide highly structured lessons to teach students a skill, for example, problem solving strategies, so that eventually the teacher can operate in a more facilitative role (i.e., quadrant 4) where students are expected to find solutions and in fact have a behavioral response repertoire for making appropriate choices.

Classroom Management Model

The model being proposed here expands the attribution theory model for helping and coping to a tri-dimensional model by adding the construct of task-relevant maturity from situational leadership style theory. The model shown in Figure 5 defines the four classroom management styles, varying attributions for student blame and control, and aligns the power and treatment styles with low task maturity and the moral and facilitative styles with high task maturity. In this conceptual scheme, task maturity is defined as the student's ability to success-fully perform tasks and/or persevere toward task completion. Student-perceived task efficacy, task relevance and task meaningfulness will all influence task maturity. Task maturity might also be influenced by cultural "dissonance" such that for certain types of tasks, culture would play a part in determining the student's maturity. Hence, maturity relative to a specific task will be influenced by the student's achievement motivation, perseverance, skill level and/or perceived ability. From the student's perspective, this may be translated into self-questioning like "Why should I do this?" (achievement motivation), "Is it important?" (perseverance), "How will this help me?" (skill level), "Can I be successful at this task?" (perceived ability).

In the situational leadership component of the model as applied to the classroom, maturity can be viewed from a variety of perspectives. Any one, or a combination, of low skill level, high task difficulty, low performance expectation, and/or lack of motivation could render a student at low maturity relative to a particular classroom task or activity.

Thus, task maturity of the learner as conceptualized in this model would be variable both across type of learning task and within learning tasks. It would also be evolving; that is, as student skill-level and/or competence in task performance increases, teachers could move into a more facilitative, resource role. When student maturity as a construct is viewed as variable, the role of the teacher then becomes one of providing sufficient variation in classroom tasks so that culturally different and/or traditionally low-performing students have the opportunity to engage in tasks in which they can succeed (or even excel). For example, a low-performing student may require a greater amount of teacher direction in a reading decoding task (i.e., student is at low maturity) than when engaged in a problem-solving cooperative learning task which is not dependent on reading skill level (i.e., student is at high maturity). Conversely, a high-performing student may function at low maturity in a cooperative group structure, at least until that student's confidence in fulfilling task expectations is secured.

Brickman et al. posited in their model that helping styles in which others are held responsible are more likely to increase competence of others than models in which they are not. Thus, the moral and facilitative styles would be the classroom management styles which would increase students' sense of competence. This model of classroom management calls on teachers to make a major paradigm shift and reconceptualize maturity as variable and relative to task expectations and demands. The model also necessitates a major operational shift by calling on teachers to provide sufficient diversity in task structure and learning activities so that traditionally low-performing students have opportunities to experience success.

References

Anderson, H. (1939). The measurement of domination and of socially integrative behavior in teachers' contacts with children. *Child Development, 10,* 73-89.

Brickman, P., Rabinowitz, V. C., Karuza, J., Coates, D., Cohn, E., & Kidder, L. (1982). Models of helping and coping. *American Psychologist, 37,* 368-384.

Brophy, J. (1979). Teacher behavior and its effects. *Journal of Educational Psychology, 71,* 733-750.

Brophy, J., & Evertson, C. (1974). *Process-product correlations in the Texas Teacher Effectiveness Study: Final report (Research Report No. 74-4).* Austin: University of Texas, Research and Development Center for Teacher Education (ERIC ED 091 094).

Brophy, J., & Good, T. L. (1986). Teacher behavior and student achievement. In M.C. Wittrock (Ed.), *Third handbook on research on teaching* (pp. 328-375). New York: Macmillan.

Charles, C. M. (1989). *Building classroom discipline.* New York: Longman.

Chrystal, C. A. (1988). Teacher management and helping style: How can we develop student self-concept? *Focus on Exceptional Children, 21,* 9-14.

Crocker, R. K., & Brooker, G. M. (1986). Classroom control and student outcomes in grades 2 and 5. *American Educational Research Journal, 23,* 1-11.

Dunkin, M., & Biddle, B. (1974). The study of teaching. New York: Holt, Rinehart and Winston.

Flanders, N. A. (1967). Teacher influence in the classroom. In E. J. Amidon & J. B. Hough (Eds.), *Interaction analysis: Theory, research and application.* Reading, MA: Addison-Wesley.

Gage, N. (1978). *The scientific basis of the art of teaching.* New York: Teachers College Press, Columbia University.

Gersten, R., Woodward, J., & Darch, C. (1986). Direct instruction: A research-based approach to curriculum design and teaching. *Exceptional Children, 53*(1), 17-31.

Gordon, T. (1974). *Teacher effectiveness training.* New York: Peter H. Wyden.

Grossman, H. (1990). *Trouble-free teaching: Solutions to behavior problems in the classroom.* Mountain View, CA: Mayfield.

Hersey, P., & Blanchard, K. H. (1972). *Management of organizational behavior: Utilizing human resources* (2nd ed.). Englewood Cliffs, NJ: Prentice-Hall.

Kounin, J. (1970). *Discipline and group management in classrooms.* New York: Holt, Rinehart and Winston.

Larrivee, B. (1985). *Effective teaching for successful mainstreaming.* New York: Longman.

Larrivee, B. (1992). *Strategies for effective classroom management.* Boston, MA: Allyn and Bacon.

Lewin, K., Lippitt, R., & White, R. (1939). Patterns of aggressive behavior in experimentally created "social climates." *Journal of Social Psychology, 10,* 271-299.

Medley, D. (1977). *Teacher competency and teacher effectiveness: A review of process-product research.* Washington, DC: American Association of Colleges for Teacher Education.

Rosenshine, B. (1979). Content, time, and direct instruction. In P. Peterson & H. Walberg (Eds.), *Research on teaching: Concepts, findings, and implications.* Berkeley, CA: McCutcheon.

Rosenshine, B., & Berliner, D. C. (1978). Academic engaged time. *British Journal of Teacher Education, 4,* 3-15.

Rosenshine, B., & Stevens, R. (1984). Classroom instruction in reading. In D. Pearson (Ed.), *Handbook of research on teaching.* New York: Longman.

Slavin, R. E., Karweit, N. L., & Madden, N. A. (1989). *Effective programs for students at risk.* Boston, MA: Allyn and Bacon.

Soar, R. S., & Soar, R. M. (1979). Emotional climate and management. In P. L. Peterson & H. J. Walberg (Eds.), *Research on teaching: Concepts, findings, and implications* (pp. 97-119). Berkeley, CA: McCutcheon.

Withall, J. (1949). The development of a technique for the measurement of social-emotional climate in classrooms. *Journal of Experimental Education, 17,* 347-361.

The following paper suggests that there may be a critical link between a fragmented curriculum and a fragmented, dispassionate view towards others. By severing not only subject matter, but emotions and depth of understanding from learning, students are deprived of opportunities to make rich, meaningful connections. Such connections are seen as the central element in developing learners with compassion, personal interdependence and tolerance for multiple perspectives.

INTEGRATED EDUCATION
FOR HUMAN RIGHTS
Todd Jennings

Introduction

Recent research (Jennings, 1991, 1993) suggests that there are two psychological characteristics conducive to responding to the needs of those outside one's own group whose human rights are being denied. The first is a recognition of one's interdependence with those outside one's own group. A second is an emotional bond or sense of connection with those whose rights are abridged, even though one may not know them personally. Integrative education admits of many articulations, but at least two of these may promote character-istics associated with acting on behalf of those outside one's own group. The first is the integration of academic disciplines, usually referred to as "interdisci-plinary study." The second is the integration of subjectivity and emotion with classroom practice.

Interdisciplinary Study

Berman (1990) claims that:

each of us develops a relationship to society and the world. Furthermore, the way we give meaning to this relationship determines the nature of our participation in the world. . . . Like a relationship with another person, our relationship with society includes such powerful factors as interconnection, emotion, influence, and vulnerability. (p. 5)

As mentioned above, research findings suggests that a critical component of human-rights advocacy is an understanding of one's interdependence with those outside one's own group, including victims of oppression. Interviews with human-rights advocates elicited rationales such as the following offered by a young woman working on behalf of those in other countries being tortured and imprisoned without due process. She says: "Part of my identity is definitely being aware that our being does impact others and theirs does ours" (Jennings, 1993).

Characteristically in the United States, societal values have not promoted a view of the world as an interdependent system. Rather, societal values have emphasized autonomy and independence (Bellah et al., 1985). Education has embodied these values by structuring classrooms and curricula to separate the disciplines and "fracture" learning into discrete disciplines and skills (Oliver, 1989). However, if students construct their understanding of the world based in part upon their educational experiences, to teach the separation of disciplines is to reap a world view characterized by segregation. The lessons we unwittingly teach by artificially segregating the disciplines manifest themselves in the ease with which students ignore interdependence and disassociate their actions from the lives and needs of others. Unless educational contexts encourage students to explore interdependence (i.e., the interdependence of the disciplines) they may never come to see themselves as interdependent. As Dewey claimed, "we never educate directly, but indirectly by means of the environment" (1966, p. 19).

Self-definition is constructed out of our investigation and internalization of our social contexts. A learning context rooted in a separatist curriculum yields a separatist and alienated sense of self. However, a learning context rooted in curricular experiences which highlight interdependence yields a self understood and experienced as interdependent and intricately related to others within the whole.

Student experiences should not be divided into unnatural disciplinary units like math, science, and reading. Rather, instruction should be organized around overarching questions which tie together the disciplines and their basic skills. Oliver suggests that we work

> toward a sophisticated theory of deep knowing and being that will raise the most general questions about the quality and destiny of the human species. . . . It is at this point, for example, that the distinction between the various academic disciplines must break down. For the study of such questions requires that we be able to move between and interrelate the fields of physics, biology, religion, history, and poetry in a single conversation. (Oliver, 1989, p. 30)

Inquiry highlighting interdependence is organized using specific student questions rather than into discrete disciplines or skills. Educators should make conscious efforts to help students explore the relationships between content areas and highlight how the various disciplines must be integrated in the process of exploring problems and their solutions.

When interdisciplinary study is an organizing principle of an educational context, themes of interdependence are more likely to be pervasive elements of students' lived experience. Consequently, the understanding of interdependence extends beyond the superficial and is understood at the level of self-definition. This is the level Caine and Caine (1991) refer to as "deep meaning." That is, the level at which information is enmeshed with emotion and purpose. In the case of my research with advocates, this "deep meaning" was evidenced by advocates' self-definitions as part of interdependent, interconnected wholes.

Subjectivity/Emotion and Instruction

Jane Roland Martin (1985) argues that "reasoned deliberation rather than spontaneous reaction, dispassionate inquiry rather than emotional response, abstract analytic theorizing rather than concrete storytelling" (p. 73) are all values passed to us from Plato, further reinforced by Modernity, and embodied in the more recent Essentialist movement. These values contribute to the severing of emotion and subjectivity from formal education. The educational impact of this value orientation are classrooms void of opportunities for emotional connection, empathic interdependence, and the development of tolerance for multiple perspectives. Martin (1985) further suggests that emotion and feeling must be "viewed as positive rather than untrustworthy elements of personality" (Martin, 1985, p. 80). To achieve this value re-orientation, activities which embody these elements must be given value in the curriculum.

However, education in the United States has tending to denigrate and discourage subjective knowing (Belenky et al., 1986, Poplin, 1988). That is, a type of knowing which relies on the personalized interpretation of curriculum content. Poplin asserts that:

> the absence . . . of a serious discussion of the subjective, the personal, the social, the interpersonal, and the passionate leaves practicing educators somewhat "languageless" in discussing their very real concerns and needs . . . In our failure to take seriously the examination of values beyond the personal cognitive aspects and in our almost abject avoidance of anything that could be construed as "feelings" we have left intact [only] half-a-language about knowledge, education, learning, and teaching. (Poplin, in press)

Research interviews with human-rights advocates suggest that those who respond to the needs of others do so because they find it difficult to objectify victims' needs. Themes of empathy and identification were pervasive in the data and lead to the conclusion that experiencing a sense of connection with oppression victims was conducive to responding on their behalf. For example, Ellen, a woman offering legal aid to the homeless, explained her reason for advocacy:

> You become aware of your connection with other people. . . . It's not just an intellectual understanding, I mean, your happiness and

sense of well-being is connected as well, that's part of the
connection. It's not just an abstract, intellectual connection with
others of your species. (Jennings, 1991, p. 87)

Notice that Ellen did not cite the rationality of her reasons, but rather a
subjective sense of her connection to people.

If responding to the needs of others requires that one subjectively
experience a sense of connection with oppression victims, then education to
promote a concern for human rights must also allow students to trust their
subjective experiences. In short, education must facilitate and validate a type of
knowing which incorporates a personalized interpretation of curriculum content
and an emotional connection with the images and subjects being investigated.
When educators revere objective over subjective knowledge, students are
socialized to conclude that intellectual rigor necessitates the objectification of
what/who is being studied. As a result, students apply this same mode of
understanding to images of those suffering. The result is an objectification and
dispassionate distancing of themselves from the images of those denied their
rights.

One mechanism for counteracting the objectification of those in need is
to counteract the objectification of curriculum content. Rather than promote
disassociation, curriculum can be used to promote subjective analysis and the
exploration of relational themes. For example, literature can be used to heighten
students' empathic and perspective-taking skills. Through literature, students can
be

encouraged to view problems, themes, concerns and concepts
from the perspective of different cultural groups. For example,
students might study the American Revolution from the points of
view of Anglo revolutionaries, Anglo loyalists, African Ameri-
cans, Indians, the French, and the British. (Rasinski & Padak,
1990, p. 577)

Utilized across the curriculum, literature "tells the stories of human events and
the human condition and not simply the facts, literature does more than change

minds; it changes people's hearts. And people with changed hearts are people who can move the world" (Rasinski & Padak, 1990, p. 580).

A concern for human rights is facilitated by providing students with emotionally visceral opportunities to explore their responsibilities to those whom they do not know personally. However, it is important to make such experiences critical to curriculum design and not simply token attempts given only passing attention or treated as "add-ons." Subjective analysis needs to be an organizing principle of curriculum and planning. Emotionally experienced knowledge, rather than simply didactically dispensed information, is a critical component to the promotion of a concern for the rights of others. Social consciousness arises as people interact subjectively and emotionally to name the events, relationships, and entities in their own contexts and attempt to connect with the situations of others. Subjectivity is crucial to the process of reflection and learning for the liberation of self and others.

Conclusion

In conclusion, separatism and the objectification of others are antithetical to human-rights advocacy. Undoubtedly students structure their world views and their self-concepts relative to the educational contexts in which they learn. When teaching is primarily through didactic instruction and is organized into discrete disciplines, students construct world views in mirrored response. The claims of this paper are that education currently embodies the segregation of knowledge into disciplines and values objective knowing over subjective interpretation and understanding. In doing so, educators may unwittingly equip students with the skills and values necessary to more easily separate themselves from the needs of others. The images of the oppressed become distant "objects" of study rather than compelling images which are allowed to capture students and to which students feel compelled to respond and acknowledge their interdependency. To the extent that education continues to focus on segregated disciplines and ignore the interdisciplinary nature of knowledge, the

> educated person will be provided with knowledge about others, but will not be taught to care about their welfare or to act kindly toward them. That person will be given some understanding of society, but will not be taught to feel injustices. . . . [They will be] one who can reason but has no desire to solve real problems in the real world. (Martin, 1985, p. 73)

References

Belenky, M. F., Clinchy, B. M., Goldberger, N. R. & Tarule, J. M. (1986). *Women's ways of knowing.* New York: Basic Books.

Bellah, R., Madsen, R., Sullivan, W., Swidler, A., Tipton, S. (1985). *Habits of the heart: Individualism and commitment in American life.* New York: Harper and Row.

Berman, S. (1990). The real ropes course: The development of social consciousness. *The Educating for Social Responsibility Journal* (pp. 1-18). Cambridge: Educators for Social Responsibility.

Caine, R. N. & Caine, G. (1991). *Making connections: Teaching and the human brain.* Alexandria, VA: Association for Supervision and Curriculum Development.

Dewey, J. (1966). *Democracy and education: An introduction to the philosophy of education.* New York: The Free Press.

Jennings, T. (1991). *The psychological nature of social consciousness: Motivations and the nature of self.* Unpublished doctoral dissertation, The Claremont Graduate School, Claremont, California.

Jennings, T. (1993). *[Explorations into the psychology of human-rights advocacy].* Unpublished raw data.

Martin, J. (1985). Becoming educated: A journey of alienation or integration. *Journal of Education, 167* (3), 71-84.

Oliver, D. (1989). *Education, modernity, and fractured meaning.* New York: SUNY Press.

Poplin, M. (1988). Holistic/constructivist principles of the teaching/learning process: Implications for the field of learning disabilities. *Journal of Learning Disabilities, 21,* 401-416.

Poplin, M. (in press). Feminist pedagogy and the non-cognitive in the classroom. *Proceedings from the Culverhouse Conference on Changing Paradigms in Special Education.* University of Southern Florida.

Rasinski, T. & Padak, N. (1990). Multicultural learning through children's literature. *Language Arts, 67,* 576-580.

The term "Integrative learning" refers to a complex system of providing school education that makes better sense to students. Many of the articles included in this collection have described ways to approach integrative curriculum and learning. This author provides good direction in integrating services for the school. The Comer model and the Edmonds model are used to illustrate ways in which service integration can take place. As well, an interesting case study, detailing the author's experiences in initiating service integration, is included.

THE MOSAIC OF URBAN EDUCATION:
A CASE DESCRIPTION
Richard K. Gordon

My attendance at a parochial school led me to believe some unsavory things about my public school friends. I believed that many of them were poorly educated because their teachers were poorly trained. I also believed that they would never achieve as well as I and my parochial school companions because of a lack of motivation and direction in their studies. I thought that these students were suffering in an educational environment which had coldly extinguished the spark of humanness given to them at birth. I believed that public schools were the worst possible places for children to go to learn and I was determined to remain in my parochial setting. After high school graduation I began to realize that many of my misconceptions were the result of the religious instruction which I received. This emphasized the righteousness of religion over the heathenism of secular instruction. Unfortunately, however, I found that many of the images that I had of the urban public school were frighteningly accurate.

Many problems found in urban city public schools are not new (Ornstein, 1975). Issues surrounding school desegregation, test scores, violence and discipline, teacher effectiveness, and curriculum relevance come to a head in the inner cities of many urban areas. Typically, these schools have a large number of minority students, and students who speak languages other than English. Large percentages of parents are not typically found at the school on back-to-school night. These students, when compared to their small city or suburban cohorts, usually are guilty or have been accused of various and more frequent school misdemeanors by teachers and administrators. Many students experience aspects of gang violence and drug lifestyles. Often, talk of future achievement in school is reserved for children who might be called "squares" by their non-academically oriented peers.

One depiction of urban school life can be seen in feature film presentations. In the pseudo-biographical movie "Lean on Me" tough school principal Mr. Joe Clark eliminates the chaotic conditions in an urban high school. He is praised for his efforts by the secretary of education. Another film "Stand and Deliver" illustrates the above-average teaching efforts of Mr. Jaime Escalante. These endeavors were necessary to help his urban students attain superior scores on a standardized achievement measure.

These films depict a model of the tough overseer or the teacher of superior wisdom and insight as possible architects for urban school reform. Fortunately, for those educators not possessed of the battlefield charisma of Mr. Clark or the martyr-like (at least as depicted in the film portrayal) personality of Mr. Escalante, other methods of urban school reform are much more sanguine. These models, which clearly define successful strategies for changing urban schools, can be found in educational research. Following are two such paradigms.

The effective schools model championed by Dr. Ronald Edmonds (1986, p. 93) has five factors which have been found in successful urban schools with large numbers of poor and minority youth. These correlates of effective schools are:

1.   Principals of effective schools are instructional leaders.

2. Adults in the school know the instructional emphasis and institutional mission of the school.

3. Effective schools are safe, clean, orderly, and quiet.

4. Teachers expect high academic achievement from their students.

5. Standardized achievement tests are used as a basis of program evaluation.

These characteristics can be transferred to other schools needing a reform intervention strategy.

The second model is given by Dr. James Comer (1988) of Yale University. He has developed a model termed the School Development Program (SDP) composed of four centers of focus which have been strongly associated with his intervention activities leading to urban school reform:

1. a school governance and management team,

2. a mental health team,

3. a parent's team,

4. a team responsible for social projects.

These researchers have worked with successful and failing urban schools and school districts and they have developed and implemented their interventions. Use of their strategies has led to an overall change in the academic and social environment of the schools where put into action.

This paper describes the adaptation and implementation of the SDP, specifically, and the effective schools research, generally, to one public urban elementary school. In his research, Comer (Comer, 1980; Clark, 1983) describes urban schools that have had a history of failing. The school that is the focus of this report had not developed any history whatsoever. Its image was not encumbered with perceptions of student failures and unsafe learning conditions. There was no history of this type for the school because it had just reopened. The effective schools research by Edmonds had data on schools identified with appreciable histories of failure.[1] This ahistorical variable helped in the generation of a creative and unusual implementation of the Comer and Edmonds research findings and policy recommendations that address the phenomena of urban public schooling.

While this school did not have the image of a failing school, many of the first cadre of students had come from institutions where they had experienced academic failure. Many had arrived at the new site with cumulative records that showed that they had experienced discipline problems. Also in attendance were children who presented to the school academic records and personal social histories which were stellar.

A month prior to the 1989 school year I was approached by the school principal to discuss her plans to promote school success. At our initial meeting we discussed several avenues and approaches to school improvement and settled on implementing the SDP with modifications as explained below. Essentially, our plan involved promoting a school climate supportive of and committed to superior academic achievement and personal success. This commitment to school success has been continually reinforced, as evidenced, for example, in opening school ceremonies, where all the speakers articulated the importance of this theme.

A Modified "School Development Program"

Dr. James P. Comer's model (1988) for addressing the educational failure of minority youth in urban schools consists of four major components (listed above). School administrative personnel, mental health consultants, and teachers participate on the governance and mental health components while parents and some members of the former groups participate in the social projects and in the parent's component.

For purposes of the current project, modifications occurred along several of these components. For example, in the initial organizational plan funds were not available to hire mental health personnel. Therefore personnel already on site needed to be used to fulfill the requirements of this component. In my case, with a background in educational psychology I was responsible for dealing with students in need of counseling. Eventually the school district was able to provide outside consultation.

The overriding goal of the principal was to promote and enhance the developing image of the school. A project was developed to design a Health Science magnet school, thereby meeting the "Special Projects" aspect of the SDP. This particular "Special Project" component was one way to promote the image of academic success. It was also seen as a means of attracting children from outside the attendance zone. Additionally, many on the Special Projects Advisory Committee saw that having an elementary magnet school that promoted the health sciences would positively impact the community overall as well as individual student self-perception.

Health Sciences Magnet School

The development of a magnet school for the health sciences did not occur by chance. The elementary school is very close to the local community hospital, which has "adopted" the school. Second, the school has been named after a prominent African-American physician from the area who was the first of his race to receive privileges at this community hospital. There is also an inestimable amount of curriculum revenue to be found and mined within the context of the Health Sciences. This choice, to develop a magnet school in the Health Sciences seemed to be very reasonable.

The initial development meetings for this project took place at California State University, San Bernardino. It was here that faculty members representing Health Sciences, Nursing and Education met with the administrative staff of the elementary school. At this meeting it was decided to contact the Riverside county department of education's "Healthy Schools" program development officer who was working directly with the State Department of Education on the development of a curriculum identified as "Healthy Kids-Healthy California" (California, 1989).

This instructional model was not a self-contained course of study. Instead it was conceived as having eight separate health related components. These were addressed through several curricula avenues. The "Healthy Kids-Healthy California" framework provided for the health sciences magnet development team a structure with which to organize a comprehensive curriculum to guide the health science magnet program. The initial organizational meeting was followed by many more during the school term.

By June the Health Sciences committee had accomplished its task. The magnet school has been listed in the school district bulletin identifying magnet school choices. To reach this point the special projects health sciences committee tapped individual resources from a variety of areas. This collective action from individuals and groups not directly connected with the school marked a minor yet important change from the "SDP." These persons will continue to participate in the Health Sciences Project. They may be asked to participate in other projects or on other advisory committees as the need arises. They form a cadre of support that can assist the school in accomplishing its mission on an as needed basis. While the Health Sciences advisory committee focused on its particular objective, continuing attention was also devoted to other aspects of the principal's vision contained within the "SDP."

Student Mental Health

In the "SDP" school mental health professionals as a team screen children having emotional, learning or behavioral problems. A coordinated effort was not implemented in this current approach. Instead, in September I asked teachers to select students that they felt exhibited frequent maladaptive behaviors for participation in counseling sessions. I began with two groups of seven students each. There were seven second and third graders and seven fourth and fifth graders. While no specific criteria were articulated to the teachers for referral purposes there did appear to be one factor that all of these students had in common. This factor was that their teachers perceived them to be defiant.

Our initial counseling sessions got under way for forty-five minutes once a week. We met five times. A natural break point occurred during the Christmas holidays. After the vacation period a mental health team, consisting of two persons, hired by the school district, was assigned to service the entire student body in a variety of areas. These areas included self-esteem counseling, drug and gang counseling, and any acute cases of distress. One member of this service was also to take over the two groups who were in counseling before the Christmas break.

A look at census information for this population tract indicated that the school had in attendance children who were having debilitating home and community experiences. While one may be aware of the academic picture describing many inner city neighborhoods it is much more graphic to be working with children who form the descriptions. The effects of abuse, lack of food, parental separation, and meager incomes are all too evident. The mental health component of the SDP attempts to address the psycho-social outcomes presented by these needs.

At the elementary school, it was decided to let one member of the behavioral consulting firm address the most severe needs of the student population. The other member of the staff was to continue with school-wide and group counseling.

The latter consultant introduced the "Heres Looking at You 2000" course of study. This self-esteem curriculum was given to the entire school once a week. The small group counselor was also given instructions on how to implement an assertive discipline program. The facility of the assertive model in establishing clear baseline behavior for the students was one reason why it was selected. The counselor was to use this strategy while concurrently developing student self-esteem through the packaged program.

The students receiving attention from the other consultant presented home situations which required immediate attention from outside social service agencies. It is my opinion that there may be other children in the school who would also benefit from such services. The children who did receive help were the "behavior problems." As such they were already isolated and under scrutiny.

Now that there were mental health professionals at the school, weekly meetings to discuss student behaviors were set. This tactic was in line with the Comer model. These weekly meetings were to be held among the members of the mental health team and the school governance team. Our agenda included discussion of students who had discipline referrals during the week and the outcomes of intervention strategies for these students. We also were to fine-tune school-wide discipline intervention strategies. Because of the difficulty in gathering the principle players together during the school day these meetings were partially effective in addressing the proposed agenda. The Mental Health strategy was expected, as in the Comer model, to be a major component of the overall program. In our case, several aspects coalesced contributing to a less than powerful aspect of the program when compared to our Special Projects activity.

A smooth transition of counselors to the two small student groups that began in November was not achieved. Many original group children were not seen again by a counselor for the remainder of the school year. The outside consultant had never worked with school-aged children and had trouble delivering the assertive model. The "Here's Looking at You 2000" curriculum was also encumbered with the lack of teaching/school experience of the counselor. While this paucity of experience was not the only reason for the generally anemic performance of the mental health component of the process, scheduling activities, the unavailability of key personnel are additional reasons why the component faltered, it was certainly a major factor to its jagged implementation.

The senior mental health counselor continued work with students with extreme needs. The school received a community outreach worker who handled the discipline referrals. This worker became a member of the mental health team and was made aware of the intervention efforts that had already taken place. However, she was not fully integrated into the program until after two months of work. Her work relieved much of the burden on the principal who before this time handled most of the student discipline referrals.

The benefits to be derived from the mental health component are very obvious. Besides identifying students coming from dysfunctional families, other students with special needs were also identified. For example, it was learned that one student in the small counseling groups had been, when he was younger, in a coma because of a swimming accident. This student was on the bottom of a pool for five minutes. This accident would appear to be significant and demanding of attention during his early school years. Until being identified in the third grade because of his behavior he had not received any special academic assistance or cognitive testing. An IEP was conducted and he is now out of the regular education program and receiving instruction that reflects his unique needs. Similarly other students were receiving special help from several sources which they would not have otherwise been granted. As the project continues this aspect of the effective schools strategy will continue to become strengthened.

In a personal correspondence with Dr. Comer, he suggests that the problems being experienced in the mental health area are typical of a first year program. In urban schools it is not uncommon to have wide variations in student achievement and behavior. This is certainly the case at this elementary school. Here, our mental health effort was directed at extreme cases of maladaptive/anti-social behavior. It seemed necessary, however, that to integrate the mental health component within the much larger model requires significant resources and organization. These students have a cornucopia of good and negative behaviors and experiences which are not typically found in non-urban city schools. To unlock their learning potential a global assessment of their psychological, social, academic, and spiritual health may be required.

Academic Enrichment[2]

Students who were described as marginal, that is, their academic and social skills were seen as borderline between potential failure and potential success were identified by their teachers. Five fifth grade students meeting this description were selected to receive academic enrichment and tutoring. They were to receive basic academic and speaking skills instruction. This latter aspect of their training was to prepare them for a visit to a class of preservice teachers at the university.

Students taking a class in educational psychology prepared for the visit by reading a chapter in their text on minority students. Many university students were unfamiliar with the learning characteristics of minority students as described in their text. In the class the elementary students would discuss with university students aspects of urban school education and life in an urban environment. In many cases this discussion would be the only experience these university students will have on the topic of urban school education before entering the teaching profession. The discussion was to be used as a forum for both groups to become aware of each other's experiences that effect the teacher learner process.

The elementary students prepared for the visit for ten weeks with a university undergraduate student intern in sociology. She worked with five fifth grade students two to three times per week at one and one-half hours per session. Students and the intern worked together on public speaking and interviewing skills. The intern also devoted time to work with the students on basic academic skills which were a part of the standardized test activity which all students took.

Before meeting with the students the student intern met with the investigator to be briefed on the academic achievement of the children, salient characteristics of the school and instructional strategies. As the encounter with the university students was approaching the intern helped the elementary students compose questions they would like to ask the prospective teachers. The meeting took place after the university students read a chapter in their educational psychology text book (Biehler & Snowman, 1990) on the "disadvantaged student." After the session both groups expressed sincere remarks about the genuineness of the experience.[3] Many of the university students questioned the description of the "underclass" student that they had read in their text.

Another group of similar students was identified by the school resource teacher. She selected ten students who were brought to the university to learn how to use a computer drawing program. This one and a half hour exercise was coupled with a tour of the campus. These students also expressed a desire to return to the campus.

Additional activities such as the Standard English Program which assists students in enhancing their verbal and speaking skills was in place at the school. Students in this program participated in a oratorical contest and one student placed second in a district-wide competition. This program was not integrated into the fabric of the adapted SDP. It illustrates however the many puzzle pieces that need to fit in a successful urban public school that provide academic enrichment and ancillary training out of classroom and beyond the normal school day services to youth.

Summary

Developing a positive urban school ambiance requires efforts which must be exerted at several social, academic and political levels. The academic aspect of this equation has been given in part by Drs. Comer and Edmonds. The "SDP" with its four elements:

1.   a school governance and management team

2.   a mental health team

3.   a parent's team

4.   a team responsible for social projects

and the five correlates of the effective schools model of Edmonds:

1.   Principals of effective schools are instructional leaders.

2.   Adults in the school know the instructional emphasis and institutional mission of the school.

3.   Effective schools are safe, clean, orderly, and quiet.

4.   Teachers expect high academic achievement from their students.

5.   Standardized achievement tests are used as a basis of program evaluation.

provide strategies for academic and social interventions in large urban schools which have been shown empirically to lead to positive improvements. However, social and political images of life in urban schools are not neutral.

They can be depicted as tough institutions where super teachers and macho administrators get results. Or, they can be seen as institutions just like many others; some are successful and some are not. What makes the urban school an interesting phenomenon to study is that we know that so many are not performing at a socially acceptable level. Not all are failing, and as Edmonds and Comer have pointed out we can learn from the successful occurrences.

The emphasis on the failure of poor and minority students in our public schools has drawn attention away from those which are successful. Causal or strong correlates of that success have been documented. By focusing on the positive aspects of urban schools we are not being overly optimistic. Problems do occur in the public schools of our metropolitan areas but from whence do they evolve?

Our first year's experience has taught us a great deal. The adaptation of the Comer model integrated with the research findings from the effective schools literature points to the direction we will continue to follow to foster a positive and meaningful image and to develop superior academic achievement in all of the children. As suggested in the description above, adaptations and unique innovations are necessary in order to evolve a model that best meets the individual needs of this school.

The social, political, and academic environment of inner cities has been well defined in the history of education. Inner city urban schools should not, however, be synonymous with low achievement and other ills. Oakes (1985) notes that the low achievement of the 1900 "new immigrants" marked school conditions similar to what we find today in our urban schools. Positive change models do exist. Two have been cited herein. The work described has illustrated how these urban education intervention models can be manipulated to address specific needs of specific schools. Research data is forthcoming that illuminates, empirically, the events presently described descriptively at the school site.

The situation of the urban school can be likened a mosaic. Many elements in the children's lives, the organization of the school, the influence of historical and social phenomena all center in one area called school. Placing the pieces of the mosaic in a coherent fashion is an art. Anyone wishing to participate in the process must be very sensitive to the many pieces of the mosaic which give it unique characteristics. Holding these images in mind can aid in developing school intervention models which proffer significant returns in academic success and more importantly human development.

Endnotes

[1]Effective schools are described by Edmonds as those where the proportion of low-income children demonstrating academic mastery is virtually identical to the proportion of middle-class children who do so.

[2]A more detailed description of these activities is being prepared for another publication.

[3]The interview activity was done twice. The second one did not generate the enthusiasm of the first. A more specific account of the activities will be presented later in another document.

References

Biehler, R. F., & Snowman, J. (1990). *Psychology applied to teaching* (6th ed.). Boston: Houghton Mifflin.

California State Department of Education. (1989, April). *Healthy Kids-Healthy California.*

Clark, R. (1983). *Family life and school achievement: Why poor black children succeed or fail.* Chicago: University of Chicago Press.

Comer, J. (1980). *School power: Implications of an intervention project.* New York: Free Press.

Comer, J. (1988). Educating poor minority children. *Scientific American, 259*(5), 42-48.

Edmonds, R. (1986). Characteristics of effective schools. In U. Neisser (Ed.), *The school achievement of minority children* (p. 93). New Jersey: Lawrence Earlbaum.

Oakes, J. (1985). *Keeping track: How schools structure inequality.* New Haven, CT: Yale University Press.

Ornstein, A., Levine, D., & Wilkerson, D. (1975). *Reforming metropolitan schools.* Pasadena: Goodyear Publishing Company, pp. 5-31.

Embracing a need for improvement in science education, the author focuses on improvement of the preparation of elementary science educators. This article contains a comprehensive overview of a variety of educational approaches, details the nature of science education, and provides assistance with development of inquiry teaching strategies.

IMPROVING SCIENCE EDUCATION:
AN INTEGRATIVE APPROACH

Joseph Jesunathadas

Introduction

The current literature on the status of precollege science education is for the most part negative. Achievement scores indicate that our students lag behind in the sciences when compared to students of comparable ages from other countries such as South Korea, Japan, and Germany (Mullis & Jenkins, 1988). There is also evidence that many students have negative attitudes toward science (Yager & Yager, 1985). The decline in the quality of science education can be attributed to a number of factors ranging from assigning teachers with inadequate preparation in the content of science to inadequate funding or facilities for science activities (Harms & Yager, 1981; Stake & Easley, 1978).

At the elementary school level there is a general reluctance among teachers to teach science. In many schools it is quite common for teachers to allocate the least amount of time for science (Cawelti & Adkinson, 1985; Goodlad, 1984; Harms & Yager, 1981; Mechling & Oliver, 1983; Stake & Easley, 1978). Teachers' self-reports indicate that many of them prefer to teach other subjects over science (Czerniak, 1983; Czerniak & Chiarelott, 1985; Harms & Yager, 1981).

Improving the condition of science education has been the focus of a variety of change agencies for almost three decades. Launching of Sputnik in 1957 sparked many to examine and make efforts to improve the condition of science education. Though the intensive efforts of dedicated science educators have brought about many changes, particularly curricular changes, science education is still in need of much improvement.

In this article, I have described some of the areas I consider important for bringing meaningful changes in elementary science education. Specifically described are the teachers' (a) knowledge of the content and process skills of science, (b) understanding of the nature of science, (c) understanding of the nature of the learner, and (d) knowledge of and skills in the methods of science teaching. A survey of the science education research literature is indicative of the importance of each of the above elements to successful science teaching.

Though each area has been addressed separately, successful change is more effectively brought about if an integrative approach is implemented. Teacher development programs that integrate such important elements are more likely to result in positive long-term changes than those that address piece-meal changes. An integrative approach is more efficient in addressing the inter-relationships among the various areas and in making evident commonalities. Focusing on any one of these areas in the absence of others often does not lead to lasting changes. The situation is analogous to focusing on the trees and not seeing the forest.

Content Preparation

The teachers' reluctance to teach science is most commonly attributed to their inadequate preparation in the content and process skills of the sciences (Harms & Yager, 1981; Mechling, 1984; Stake & Easley, 1978; Weiss, 1978, 1987). Many have completed only 6 to 12 quarter hours of science as part of the liberal studies undergraduate degree requirements. Many consider such preparation superficial and insufficient to help them teach science. Furthermore, their inadequate content knowledge might also be the reason that course work in the methods of science teaching has had little impact on how they teach.

Teachers inadequately prepared in the content and processes of science are not in a position to teach science effectively. Underprepared teachers attempting to teach science face the difficulty of being unable to diagnose student misconceptions, provide suitable cues to enable students to develop alternative conceptions, or ask probing questions that help students develop science concepts (Happs, 1987). Successful teachers often have obvious strengths in their pedagogical content knowledge. Their background often enables them to give explanations that are clear and appropriate. They are also able to provide concrete real life examples and analogies to illustrate abstract concepts (Shulman, 1986). Effective teaching can only be achieved when teachers skillfully integrate their knowledge of the content and teaching methods to facilitate learning.

A variety of approaches that include hands-on learning, active demonstrations, and the use of other instructional technologies are being implemented to help teachers develop necessary and sufficient content knowledge and process skills. Such approaches, however, do not preclude the need for keeping abreast with changes in science that accrue as a result of new and more compelling evidence or new paradigms. Old theories must give way to new ones if the old is not sufficient to explain new findings. The act of learning of science content should be consistent with the very nature of science. Attitudes of skepticism, curiosity, willingness to accept change, and freedom to investigate and try new and unexplored vistas are essential to learning science.

Understanding the Nature of Science

How teachers view science is important to how and what they teach in the classroom. It is important that teachers have views of the nature of science that are consistent with those that are held by the community of scientists and science educators. The responsibility of helping students become scientifically literate and functional in a post-industrial era rests heavily on teachers who, as a group, do not appear to have an understanding of the nature of science.

I have my methods students interview elementary teachers about their perceptions of the nature of science. An important finding is the difficulty teachers have with this task. Some teachers appear not to have the words to describe the nature of science. However, many teachers describe science as a field of study about natural phenomena. Comments such as "science deals with everything in the universe" and "science deals with the earth, the moon, planets, stars, and all other natural things that surround us" were not uncommon. Such comments are encouraging because the focus of science is to understand nature.

Some teachers also focused on the notion that science includes the use of specific processes that lend legitimacy to findings. However, many perceived the "scientific method" as the only legitimate procedure in scientific investigations. Other exploratory methods were often considered with great suspicion. These findings indicate that science is often thought of as the process by which scientists accumulate information about natural phenomena and the products of such endeavors, i.e., the resulting knowledge or facts about natural phenomena.

Often missing in the teachers' definitions is the affective component associated with the endeavor of science. Though teachers make implicit reference to curiosity as an essential component of the scientific endeavor, they do not make reference to attitudes of persistence, objectivity, skepticism, and open-mindedness; and they do not address the fact that attitudes of dogmatism and authoritarianism have no place in the scientific endeavor. Teachers should be aware that the positive attitudes listed above are conducive to a realization that existing theories and explanations are tentative and subject to change in light of new and supporting evidence.

Current perceptions of the nature of science are quite different from those held around the turn of the century. Contemporary conceptions of science are more inclusive. For example, science and technology are no longer considered as distinct enterprises but rather as an integrated system driven by societal issues. Most scientific research today is oriented toward problems of human, material, or global welfare rather than on advancing new theories. The traditional disciplines of biology, physics, chemistry, and geology are not quite functional. The boundaries of science can no longer be defined by such disciplines. Science is characterized today by more specific problems of research such as fiber optics, upper atmosphere physics, seismic forecasting, or immunology rather than by the broad disciplines.

Contemporary issues are not often addressed by teachers who determine the curriculum to be used on the content of the textbooks. The science curriculum should reflect the interaction of science, technology, and society to help children function productively in modern society. This goal can only be achieved if teachers develop perceptions of science that are not traditional but reflect current changes.

Understanding the Nature of the Learner

Recently, many educators have begun to focus their efforts to understand how children construct meaning from their environment. There is consensus that children actively construct views about natural phenomena based on personal experiences and observations (Resnick, 1983). Often these views do not agree with those of trained scientists. Children do not simply assimilate what they are told or read. They actively look to make sense of the world by trying to fit previous experiences with new ones. Meaning is constructed and not implanted.

Teachers wonder why many children fail to apply facts and principles presented and drilled in class to interpret actual physical phenomena. For example, many children will agree that if two objects, one heavier than the other, are simultaneously dropped from some height, the heavier one will reach the ground before the lighter one. Such ideas are analogous to those held by Aristotle. Children respond to formal instruction in terms of their preexisting and intuitive ideas of the world. New experiences are often interpreted in light of existing conceptual frameworks.

It is interesting to note that children often agree among themselves about how the world works and give similar explanations for natural phenomena. This research finding has important implications for classroom practice. Teachers need to be alert to students' alternative explanations of natural phenomena. The alternative explanations of one or two students should be sufficient to indicate to the teachers that other students might also have similar conceptions.

Another related finding is that student explanations are often predictable. There are certain alternative conceptions that are common to most children. The example of the falling objects described above is just one of them. Teachers need to be aware of such common conceptions and be prepared to provide students ample examples and experiences to confront the alternative conceptions with more appropriate and acceptable conceptions.

However, it is important to note that children often resist changing their views of the world (this is analogous to the resistance for change that is evident in the history of science [Clement, 1983, p. 235]). Telling children the correct answers is often only temporally satisfying. Children quickly resort to their own constructed views when confronted with new situations that involve the physical principles dealt in class. Often, observations are not adequate to help children change their explanations. Helping children form world views that are consistent with views held by scientists might be facilitated by exposing them to rich scientific experiences early in their schooling. Ample time and many different experiences are necessary to help children learn science. Teachers should focus on providing children with qualitative rather than quantitative experiences. Actively acknowledging the theories children commonly hold and pitting them against those held by the scientific community is also considered a useful strategy in helping children deal with new ideas presented in class.

A further and related concern that is often not adequately addressed is the mismatch between the cognitive demands of the learning tasks and the cognitive developmental levels of the students. New teachers often have unrealistic views of children and either expect too much or too little from them. The result is that children find the tasks either uninteresting and irrelevant or too complex and discouraging. Asking primary children to give explanations for phenomena that humans have struggled with for centuries is not good pedagogy. Such questions often result in children making guesses and faking their way through. The "Why?" questions can wait for later years when the child has become familiar with many different experiences that are associated with the phenomena of interest.

An assignment that I give student teachers in their science methods course is to conduct interviews with the students they teach. A variety of Piagetian tasks are included in such interviews. A recurring finding the student teachers report is how they had misjudged the cognitive abilities of the children. Based on such findings the student teachers often make major changes in their science lesson plans. Typical changes include more hands-on activities that help students better conceptualize the science concepts. An awareness of Piaget's theory of cognitive development will help teachers make more appropriate curricular and instructional decisions. Such an awareness is more likely to result in teachers including more concrete experiences that are most suitable and enjoyable for elementary students.

Developing Teaching Strategies for Cognitive Growth

A major concern with existing science teaching strategies is that they do not reflect the spirit of "sciencing." Teaching science should help children develop science content knowledge, science process skills, and attitudes toward science that will help them meet their personal needs, effectively address societal issues, and provide adequate awareness of career choices (NSTA Position Statement on Preschool and Elementary Level Science Education, 1986). Teaching strategies that focus only on science content through the reading of textbooks and ignore doing science are most inadequate to meet such goals. Every effort should be made to move away from simply reading the textbook and answering the questions that follow at the end of the chapters.

Much effort is being expended to help teachers develop inquiry teaching strategies. In particular teachers are being widely trained in the learning cycle approach. This particular inquiry approach includes three stages: the exploration stage, the invention stage, and the extension stage. In the exploration or hands-on stage, students gather data and evidence about a specific phenomenon under investigation. In the next stage, students organized, transformed, analyzed, and interpreted the data in an effort to make sense of their investigations. That is, in the stage of invention or explanation students extract meaning and learn concepts. The third stage is when students extend their understanding of the concepts to new situations. Applying the concepts to new situations helps students see the relevance of what they learn in school.

Many teachers trained in the learning cycle approach have indicated that they find the approach not only consistent with the scientific enterprise but also interesting to the students. They have indicated that children enjoy the hands-on experiences and have better attitudes toward science. In addition to facilitating the learning of specific concepts and principles, the hands-on explorative activities stimulate a variety of critical thinking skills and science process skills.

Further investigations need to be carried out to examine how the learning cycle approach might be integrated with other instructional methods. Implementing only one approach of teaching is not only boring but also likely to be less effective. Teachers should effectively implement a variety of teaching strategies that foster the development of cognitive skills that will support them for a life long education. The recommendations for teachers from the works of Jean Piaget, Jerome Bruner, David Ausubel, Hilda Taba, and Albert Bandura to name a few, should be skillfully integrated to develop teaching strategies that effectively meet the goals of science education.

Conclusion

Developing useful teaching strategies and skillfully implementing them will help teachers develop a better sense of self-efficacy regarding science teaching. In fact, each of the areas (i.e., developing knowledge of the content and process skills of science, understanding of the nature of science, understanding of the nature of the learner, and developing knowledge of and skills in the methods of science teaching) addressed above are positively associated with developing self-efficacy about teaching science. Science teacher educators need to integrate theories of teaching and learning in the process of preparing teachers, for there is much to gain from theories other than those of Piaget or Ausubel. The integrative approach, furthermore, permits one to view the teaching/learning process as metaphors—the kaleidoscopic effect where the same pieces of glass get arranged into many different designs.

References

Cawelti, G., & Adkinson, J. (1985, April). ASCD study reveals elementary school time allocations for subject areas; other trends noted. *ASCD curriculum update*. Alexandria, VA: ASCD Publication.

Czerniak, C. M. (1983). *An investigation of the relationships among anxiety toward science and sex, grade level, and achievement in science*. Unpublished master's thesis, Bowling Green State University, Bowling Green, OH.

Czerniak, C. M., & Chiarelott, L. (1985). Science anxiety among elementary school students: Equity issues. *Journal of Educational Equity and Leadership, 5*(4), 291-308.

Goodlad, J. I. (1984). *A place called school: Prospects for the future*. New York: Macmillan.

Happs, J. (1987). Good teaching of invalid information: Exemplary junior secondary science teachers outside their field of expertise. In K. Tobin &

B. J. Fraser (Eds.), *Exemplary practice in science and mathematics teaching.* Perth: Curtin University of Technology.

Harms, N. C., & Yager, R. E. (Eds.). (1981). *What research says to the science teacher, vol. 3* (#471-14776). Washington, DC: National Science Teachers Association.

Mechling, K. R., & Oliver, D. L. (1983). *What research says about elementary school science.* Handbook. Project for promoting science among elementary school principals.

Mullis, I. V. S., & Jenkins, L. B. (1988). *The 1986 science report card: Elements of risk and recovery.* Princeton, NJ: National Assessment of Educational Progress, Educational Testing Services.

Resnick, L. B. (1983). Mathematics and science learning: A new conception. *Science, 220,* 477-478.

Shulman, L. S. (1986). Those who understand: Knowledge growth in teaching. *Educational Researcher, 15*(2), 4-14.

Stake, R. E., & Easley, J. A. (1978). *Case studies in science education.* Urbana, IL: University of Illinois, Center for Instructional Research and Curriculum Evaluation.

Weiss, I. R. (1978). *Report on the 1977 national survey of science, mathematics, and social studies education.* Research Triangle Park, NC: Center for Education Research and Evaluation.

Weiss, I. R. (1987). *1985-86 national survey of science and mathematics education.* Research Triangle Park, NC: Center for Educational Research and Evaluation, Research Triangle Institute.

Yager, R. E., & Yager, S. O. (1985). Changes in perceptions of science for third, seventh, and eleventh grade students. *Journal of Research in Science Teaching, 22*(4), 347-358.

This paper addresses the question of how the neurosciences can help to create a more informed educator. For example: If threat inhibits learning, what of tests and grades as primary motivators? If boredom creates endorphins which, literally, anesthetize the brain, what really happens in most high school classes? How could physiological differences in male and female brains give us reason to reconceptualize when and how to present science and math? Current research and thinking on topics related to education are summarized and suggestions for improving learning and memory are included.

WHAT EDUCATORS NEED TO KNOW
ABOUT THE BRAIN
Renate Nummela Caine

It is beginning to look as though educators (particularly those responsible for developing learning theory and those teaching teachers how to teach in the classroom) will have to know much more about how the brain works. This does not mean that educators have to become physiologists, but that a rudimentary understanding of the brain will allow for greater communication between neuroscientists and those responsible for directing the environment for specific learning. Such dialogue may well result in a total restructuring of how information is presented. Understanding how, when and why learning occurs from a physiological perspective will also help to identify teaching methods and strategies which are most effective.

This article examines current findings in brain research which may well challenge and expand our basic assumptions about learning.

Myths

Pribram (1971) and others (Ornstein & Sobel, 1987; Springer & Deutsch, 1985; Rosenfield, 1988) have suggested that the brain appears to be very much like a hologram, every part affects the whole, and the whole is affected by all parts. Try as we may, this continues to be an incredibly abstract principle and frustrating in a world of accountability where we expect to understand specific functions pertaining to, or emanating from, specific organisms, machines or events. Something that is everywhere and nowhere does not lend itself to writing clear behavioral objectives or step by step logic or analysis. Yet unless we understand that the brain is in fact at the very least a complex interdependent organ where isolated functions are rarely ever the responsibility of one part alone, we tend to reduce the brain to a far too simplistic model. The danger with that is that we jump to premature conclusions about one portion, only to discover a larger network later which makes our original assumptions look extremely naive.

Whatever happened to "left brain/right brain learning"?

The original research done by Sperry (1968) and summarized by others (Springer & Deutsch, 1985) involved patients with epilepsy. In an attempt to "short circuit" epileptic seizures, doctors severed the corpus callosum, the bridge which joins the left and right hemisphere of the brain. By accident (quite common in science), experimenters discovered that patients with a severed corpus callosum tended to separate specific functions like seeing an object and being able to describe it verbally. They might be able to draw an object for example, but would not be able to give a verbal description or name. Over time, researchers began to identify which hemisphere was providing what information and activity. This led to a fairly specific identification of what each hemisphere was doing and ultimately led to the logical assumption that the right hemisphere dealt primarily with intuitive, creative learning, and the left hemisphere dealt predominately with linear, abstract and verbal learning including mathematics and logic. Additionally, this led to the belief that people were either left or right hemisphere dominant and hence tended to be artistic and creative/intuitive, or logical, verbal/linear. Many tests promising to identify brain dominance flooded the country. Workshops and educational consulting centered on how to identify dominance, be sympathetic to it, teach to it, and help people to expand their non-dominant functions.

In recent years, research with individuals with an intact corpus callosum has demonstrated that there is evidence of laterality, but that the regions of the brain are so interactive that for practical purposes it is almost meaningless to describe people as left or right brain dominant. There may be a very slight degree of difference in EEG activity when measured by hemispheres, but what precisely this means is still much of a mystery.

An analogy helps to reflect the major fallacy upon which such conclusions were based. Let us imagine ourselves to be scientists of cosmic magnitude looking at a city through a powerful microscope. Let us further imagine that the city is like the brain, full of interrelated functions, activities, goals and structures. As we move our microscope over the suburbs of the city we notice that this large section is devoted to activities like sleeping and entertainment such as tennis and golf. We draw the conclusion that this part of the city deals with relaxation and creativity. As we notice the downtown professional and industrial areas we conclude that this section of town focuses on production and high activity, and adheres to more rigid standards for time and productive output.

We can only see these sides of town as having totally separate functions if we fail to notice that there is constant movement back and forth from suburbs to central city and back to suburbs. We also fail to see that there are many professional and industrial work sites within the rural areas and places for rest and relaxation within the business areas.

Just as our oversized scientist would have to discover over time, brain researchers discovered that the normal brain was not that simplistically divided. The corpus callosum tends to so integrate both left and right hemisphere learning that in the normal individual dominance accounts for little more than .01 for given tasks (Hand, 1984).

This may not mean that the division in learning styles identified by dominance theory are wrong, simply that the observed preferences require a more complex explanation.

Current thinking appears to suggest that such differences may give tentative legitimacy to research identifying different modes of thinking and learning, but may also be related to other critical theories focusing on how we store and retrieve information in memory (O'Keefe & Nadel, 1978).

Teaching the Human Brain

Why the emphasis on the brain? Why do educators need to be familiar with research on the brain when that has not been emphasized in the past? The neurosciences are made up of fields such as neurophysiology, neuroanatomy, neurochemistry and neuropsychology. Until very recently (1967) these fields focused on separate aspects of brain functioning, from molecular functioning of the brain cell to how systems of neurons interact. Most of the work done was also descriptive in nature, focusing on describing and labelling specific parts and anatomical features of the brain.

Several things occurred which caused a massive explosion in our understanding of how the brain appears to work: First, those involved in brain research began to talk with each other and exchange information which helped to expand knowledge into a larger, more comprehensive picture. Second, the interest in computers and artificial intelligence resulted in a greater interest in copying the master computer--the human brain. Third, new, highly sophisticated tools have allowed scientists to "look into" the brain and actually trace nerve impulses and identify neurotransmitters (substances responsible for passing messages from one brain cell to another) and follow their path.

What scientists can not do as yet, but hope to do in the near future, is to be able to document specific functions such as neurological cell growth and expansion in humans. The PET scan, CAP and MRI scans still can not produce the high level of resolution needed to measure such fine changes in the nervous system. This is why much of the present research and brain information comes from research on brains of animals, particularly the rat (structurally its brain is a lot like those of humans--no further comparison intended).

What is meant by brain plasticity and how does it relate to learning and teaching?

Chinese Proverb:

> *"A child's mind is like a piece of paper*
> *Upon which every passerby leaves his mark."*

One of the most exciting findings in brain research was originally reported by Marian Diamond and her colleagues at U.C. Berkeley. Over a period of roughly forty years they examined the brains of rats to study anatomical features. Quite by accident they discovered that the brains of rats living in what came to be known as "enriched" environments weighed more than brains of rats from "impoverished" environments.

Along with others (Bennett, Diamond, Krech, & Rosenzweig, 1964), Diamond et al. have since accumulated a vast amount of research which indicates that the brain will grow "physiologically" if stimulated through interaction with the environment.

They defined an enriched environment as one where rats are housed in groups of 10-12 in large cages provided with toys consisting of ladders, wheels, boxes, platforms and so on. Cages are in large, brightly lit rooms and toys are changed each day and selected from a large amount of toys. Super-enriched environments include exploratory sessions in large fields (in groups of 5 or 6) with patterns of barriers which are changed daily (1/2 hour per day). The impoverished conditions include individual cages with solid walls so that animals can not see or touch each other. Cages are in separate, quiet, dimly lit rooms. (It is also important to note that the most enriching environment for any rat appears to be its natural habitat.)

Here are some of the differences reported between rat brains of those from enriched and impoverished conditions. Rat pups growing up in enriched conditions had different brains from impoverished rats after only two weeks. They had a 10% extra thickness in the general sensory area and a 14% additional thickness in the sensory integration area (back of the brain). In adult rats placed in enriched conditions, they found a 4% change in wet weight of outer layers of the brain, 6% in thickness, and increase in enzymes dealing with transmission of impulses. Glial cells are critical to brain function in that they provide nourishment to the neurons or brain cells. To appreciate their importance, Diamond et al. (1985) report that the difference between Einstein's brain and the average human brain has been narrowed down to a much greater abundance of glial cells in his cortex. Larger numbers of glial cells appear to indicate greater usage and interaction in the brain. Brains of enriched rats also showed an increase in the diameter of blood vessels in the brain, another important source of brain cell nourishment. Animals who had lived 3/4 of their lifetime before being placed in enriched environments showed positive changes in somatosensory, frontal cortex and visual spacial areas. These differed from rat to rat, but changes showed consistent over-all growth leading to the conclusion that the brain maintains its plasticity for life.

It is apparently also possible to selectively modify one or another region of the cortex, depending upon the particular program of enrichment used.

Research is beginning to show similar patterns in humans but since human volunteers for brain dissections are hard to find, such research lags behind animal research. It does seem that humans can increase such brain functioning as memory and pattern detection with age, provided they maintain healthy functioning organs. This includes kidneys, liver, heart, G.I. tract and so on.

Hebrew Proverb:

> *"Do not confine your children to your own learning*
> *For they were born in another time."*

If brain plasticity applies to humans, why haven't we been able to significantly change I.Q. through enrichment programs?

As you probably know, enrichment programs have mixed reviews. Apparently only programs where infants are in an enriched environment, 8 hours a day, 50 weeks a year, beginning at the age of six months and continuing to kindergarten have participants showing any significant change in overall I.Q.

The problem in generalizing from rodent brain functions to human learning appears to be in the way we define "learning." When moving to conclusions about human learning from experiments with laboratory animals it is important to note that "what" is learning is not specific verbal information. Learning in humans extends from understanding abstract concepts to "awareness" of peripheral factors and stimuli such as feelings, tiredness and fatigue, interests and the like, and can include the ability to reorganize information in novel ways, detect complex patterns and relationships, and generally embrace the many levels of thinking outlined by Bloom and others.

The connection between brain growth and learning, then, is complex. Brain development encompasses much more than what is captured on an I.Q. test. Equating such data on brain growth with results on standardized measures is once again too simplistic and an inaccurate way of looking at this research. Additionally it is important to explore what is meant by enrichment. Remember that in the case of the rats, enriched environments included multisensory experiences which were enjoyable for animals to engage in, and rats were also frequently stroked by lab assistants and lived and played within supportive systems. What Dr. Diamond and her colleagues are saying is simply that the brain will be more capable without specifying exactly for what. The "what" may be a complex set of outcomes that is too broad to measure and identify at this point.

How does the brain develop and are there differences between brains
of males and females?

At birth we have literally billions of nerve cells in the brain. It is estimated that the number of possible connections between brain cells within one human brain exceeds the number of atoms in the entire universe (Ornstein & Thompson, 1984)! Beginning with birth however, many millions of brain cells begin to die out, primarily those which have not been utilized in some way. This process establishes the basic network of strengths and weaknesses for later learning and experiencing. The setting of basic patterns has been called "hard wiring." Different portions of the brain develop at different times and if a portion is not utilized or developed at the appropriate moment, other areas of the brain develop instead. An example is sight. In one experiment, one eye of a cat was covered at a critical moment in vision development, the cat lost sight in that one eye even though there was no anatomical damage to the eye itself.

The critical point is that brains develop in some sequence but are highly individualized and different in terms of timing. It is estimated that the developmental difference within any particular age group can vary by five years. In terms of education, this is one reason for establishing achievement of tasks and concepts as criteria for learning, not age or grade.

Male and female brains are in fact different and appear to develop differently and at different times. There is evidence (Epstein, 1979) that there are growth spurts similar to Piaget's model of cognitive development. These occur at slightly different times than Piaget suggested and appear to differ for males and females. For most normal children, periods of rapid brain growth tend to occur during a 6-month period followed by a slower period of growth and integration. These growth "spurts" appear to occur between the ages of 2 and 4, 6 and 8, 10 and 12+, and 14 and 16+. Girls tend to lead the way in these time periods and their growth is three times that of boys in the 10 to 12+ period. That situation is reversed between ages 14 to 16+. This kind of information has led to speculation that girls are most receptive to math and science beginning at about age 10. Since most schools appear to gear these subject areas to later ages more compatible with male development, girls may not receive the appropriate stimulation and hence development of skills necessary for functioning on abstract concepts. There are many conflicting explanations for how these differences between male and female learning actually manifest, however, and this explanation is offered only as one way of showing how brain research could offer some insight and help in designing a more appropriate curriculum.

Additional information on male and female brain development is offered by Marian Diamond (1987). For instance, females have millions more cells in a broader corpus callosum. What this means is not clear. Females tend to have a fairly uniform development of the brain, males do not. In sexually mature male rats the right hemisphere is thicker than the left. This is also true of the human male and includes particularly the visual spacial cortex. Interestingly enough, as the male rat gets older, he loses much of his asymmetry and as the female ages there is some indication of a tendency toward right hemisphere dominance like the male. If we take the ovaries out of the female, her brain will develop more like the male, and without testes, the male rat brain will reflect similar development to the female. The outer portions of the brain are extremely plastic and can therefore be changed by external experiences, interactions with the environment and changes in internal hormone levels. Administration of steroids will change brain development.

*What does brain research tell us about factors that interfere with or
inhibit learning?*

Much research focuses on functions such as memory and suggest that the
brain has at least two ways of storing information (O'Keefe & Nadel, 1978;
Pribram, 1987; Yingling, 1987). O'Keefe and Nadel describe the difference
between the memorization of discrete and abstract facts which are stored in the
"Taxon" memory systems, and learning which occurs within spacial contexts or
in relationship with other complex spacial information and are stored in the
"Locale" system. Learning involves both those systems but each system appears
to be governed by specific rules, and storage and retrieval are very different.
Multisensory "life-like" learning emphasizes the utilization of the "one-trial"
locale system. Thus remembering where we were for dinner last night brings
back floods of memories none of which had to be memorized first (Nummela
& Rosengren, 1988). Memorizing facts for a test is very different.

Yingling (1987) also supports the notion that there are at least two
systems for memory, dealing respectively with knowing "how" and knowing
"what." How does something function, vs. facts or what I know. This is similar
to O'Keefe and Nadel's concept of memory because the question of "how"
requires the storage of complex, integrated information while the question of
"what" in this mode refers to specific factors and sets of skills being stored and
recalled.

Pribram (1987) suggests that three basic physiological portions of the
sub-cortical brain are involved in the learning process. Some structures deal with
information from the outside and involve the visual and auditory cortex. Other
structures deal with internal messages such as feelings and attitudes. These
messages are translated by the somatomotor system into some form of new
product. Instruction should involve all three of these parts so he suggests that
teaching should accentuate modes of perception and lead out from the student's

own motivational system (from "educare," to lead out). Teaching is the process which should bring these things together.

Threat and Boredom

The brain appears to interpret challenge and threat differently. How these are defined by an individual brain is unique to that brain, but challenge appears to harness the capacities of the brain, and threat causes what Hart (1978) calls "downshifting" into sub-cortical structures with diminished input from the frontal cortex. Metacognition is affected as well as recall of verbal information. Under threat, the thalamus releases endorphins into the system and these both anesthetize the outer glands and keep information from going into the neocortex. This same process holds for learners who have a negative attitude, are bored or overly fatigued (McGuinness & Pribram, 1980). Additionally, threat such as exams for which the individual learner is not adequately prepared or for which the learner has developed a phobic reaction, will affect the immune system. Students have been shown to have a higher amount of colds and flu following major exams or a series of exams (Ornstein & Sobel, 1987).

Boredom is extremely destructive because it can actually "train" students to develop attentional deficits. Students learn to act out or in most cases frequently "leave the room" with their minds (through fantasy for example), paying only superficial attention to the teacher. "Discipline" problems are more likely to be the result of boring teaching which has not considered the relevance and interests of students (motivation).

What then enhances learning?

The most critically undervalued factor in educational practice has been the role of the emotions in learning. Just as boredom and threat are devastating to learning, so on the other hand, when learning promises positive experiences or pleasure, reward and/or novelty, then the new information tends to move quickly into the cortex. Hart (1978) suggests that the brain works on an emotional bias system where the very first thing the brain does is decide what it wants to learn. We pay attention to things that are novel in some form or other, personally relevant or meaningful, fun, and things where there is something "in it for us." Learning, as it is often presented, not directly and meaningfully involving the student (no matter how carefully the planned out lesson, or well placed the threat), is at its best similar to putting the foot on the gas petal and the brake at the same time. Students choose their attitudinal focus, and this fact needs to be acknowledged and addressed in education. Teaching facts is not the same as creating excitement and enthusiasm for learning. M. Diamond suggests that the greatest gift we can give learners is curiosity: "Teach the children to be curious for a lifetime and you give them one of their greatest possessions" (Diamond, 1987). Curiosity is what keeps us asking questions, and finding answers gives us brain development (both are involved).

Pribram (1987) suggests that a critical balance between what he calls "active uncertainty" and familiarity needs to be kept in learning. Students should have basic information to work with, but should always be left with a question. The active uncertainty keeps the brain actively searching and questioning. The balance between uncertainty, facts, and creating real changes in the brain is critical to good teaching and lends strong support to Bruner's discovery learning. Pribram also suggests that information needs to be reorganized in novel ways and should be presented repeatedly to students over time. How many ways can a subject be explained? demonstrated? experienced?

One of the reasons "accelerative" models of teaching include the use of music, stories, metaphors, guided imagery, etc., is because they allow for repeated exposure to thoughts, ideas, and information we wish the student to understand and learn. They, along with voice intonation, humor, appropriate expressive gestures, teacher excitement, and student involvement in role playing and creative dramatics create enriching repetition, with every variation receiving appropriate focusing and involvement by the student.

Additionally, recommendations are made to utilize student pre-attentive processes such as the relaxation response (Benson et al., 1974). These are used to prepare the learner and the environment to be optimally conducive to learning. Verbal affirmations and success imagery, "brain teasers," physical movement and the arts, are also ways to expand thinking and move from teaching "things" to complex pattern detection and discovering novel solutions. Peripheral stimuli in the environment, which are not necessarily picked up consciously, may nevertheless also have a significant impact on learning (Lozanov, 1978). However, all of these processes and activities must be meticulously orchestrated by the teacher. "Gimmicks" are tricks used out of context and it is the appropriateness of activities which results in the building and integration of learning. In addition, the sincerity and integrity of the teacher appear to be vital factors in a student's willingness to take in information and experiences.

Conclusions

Much of what good teachers already know and do is being confirmed by brain research. We know, for instance, that the brain responds positively to enjoyment and challenge. Some research, however, calls into question our most basic assumptions and indicates that even good teachers have a great deal to learn. Thus, the work on memory by O'Keefe and Nadel and others suggests that all people have much instant knowledge available, and rote learning in many circumstances may interfere with learning. The brain is extremely sophisticated. Learning and teaching therefore need to be extremely sophisticated processes. Using one approach only, such as organizing information analytically (a la Ausubel for example) may be primitive or inadequate. Above all it is clear that in addition to requiring students to "learn" prescribed material and respond to social assessment, they must have permission to choose much of their learning for themselves.

References

Bennett, E. L., Diamond, M. C., Krech, D., & Rosenzweig, M. R. (1964). Chemical and anatomical plasticity of the brain. *Science, 146,* 610-619.

Benson, H., Beary, J. F., & Carol, M. P. (1974). The relaxation response. *Psychiatry, 37,* 37-46.

Diamond, M. C. (1987, January). *For research rats and students both, does boredom limit neural growth?* Paper presented at Educating Tomorrow's Children seminar, California Neuropsychology Services, San Francisco.

Diamond, M., Scheibel, A., Murphy, G., & Harvey, T. (1985). On the brain of a scientist: Albert Einstein. *Experimental Neurology, 88,* 198-204.

Epstein, H. (1979). Growth spurts during brain development, implications for educational policy. In S. Chall & F. Mirsky (Eds.), *Education and the brain.* National Society for the Study of Education yearbook. University of Chicago Press.

Hand, J. D. (1984). Split brain theory and recent results in brain research: Implications for the design of instruction. In R. K. Bass & C. R. Dills (Eds.), *Instructional development: The state of the art, II.* Dubuque, IA: Kendall/Hunt.

Hart, L. (1978). *Human brain and human learning.* New York: Longmans, Inc.

Lozanov, G. (1978). *Suggestology and outlines of suggestopedy.* New York: Gordon and Breach.

McGuinness, D., & Pribram, K. (1980). The neuropsychology of attention: Emotional and motivational controls. In M. C. Wittrock (Ed.), *The brain and psychology.* New York: Academic Press, 95131.

Nummela, R., & Rosengren, T. (1988). The brain's routes and maps: Vital connections in learning. *NAASP Bulletin - The Journal for Middle Level and High-School Administrators, 72,* 83-86.

O'Keefe, J., & Nadel, L. (1978). *The hippocampus as a cognitive map.* New York: Oxford University Press.

Ornstein, R., & Thompson, R. (1984). *The amazing brain.* Boston: Houghton Mifflin Company.

Ornstein, R., & Sobel, D. (1987). *The healing brain.* New York: Simon and Schuster, Inc.

Pribram, K. (1971). *Languages of the brain.* Monterey, CA: Brooks/Cole.

Pribram, K. (1987, January). *A systematic analysis of brain function, learning and remembering.* Paper presented at Educating Tomorrow's Children seminar, California Neuropsychiatry Services, San Francisco.

Rosenfield, I. (1988). *The invention of memory.* New York: Basic Books Inc.

Springer, S., & Deutsch, G. (1985). *Left brain, right brain.* New York: W. H. Freeman and Company.

Sperry, R. W. (1968). Hemisphere disconnection and unity in conscious awareness. *American Psychologist, 23,* 723-33.

Yingling, C. (1987, January). *Neuroscience, cognitive science, and education: Partners in progress or strange bedfellows?* Paper presented at Educating Tomorrow's Children seminar, California Neuropsychology Services, San Francisco.